The HOT BOOK of
CHILIES

Special thanks go to Derryck Strachan (Ashburton Cookery School) and Chilli Pepper Pete (retailer of fine dried chilies and hot spicy pickles), who put up with my questions and visits, as well as Andy Teo, whose cooking is always a delight to sample. Most of all, I wish to thank my wife, Sonia, and my family—Nick, Jason, Lizzi, and Antony—who have tasted and tested countless recipes, and my mother, Edna, without whom there would have been many more mistakes in the text.

The HOT BOOK of
CHILIES

History, Science, 51 Recipes, and
97 Varieties from Mild to Super Spicy

DAVID FLOYD

COMPANIONHOUSE
BOOKS

The Hot Book of Chilies, 3rd Edition

CompanionHouse Books™ is an imprint of Fox Chapel Publishers International Ltd.

Project Team
Vice President–Content: Christopher Reggio
Editor: Colleen Dorsey
Copy Editor: Anthony Regolino
Book Designer: Mary Ann Kahn
Book Layout: John Hoch

Certain recipes taken from: Asian Food (2005). © Solomon, Charmaine. Sydney: New Holland Publishers (Australia) Pty Ltd

ISBN 978-1-62008-376-5

The Cataloging-in-Publication Data is on file with the Library of Congress.

Fox Chapel Publishing
903 Square Street
Mount Joy, PA 17552

Fox Chapel Publishers International Ltd.
7 Danefield Road, Selsey (Chichester)
West Sussex PO20 9DA, U.K.

www.facebook.com/companionhousebooks

We are always looking for talented authors. To submit an idea, please send a brief inquiry to acquisitions@foxchapelpublishing.com.

Printed and bound in China
22 21 20 19   2 4 6 8 10 9 7 5 3 1

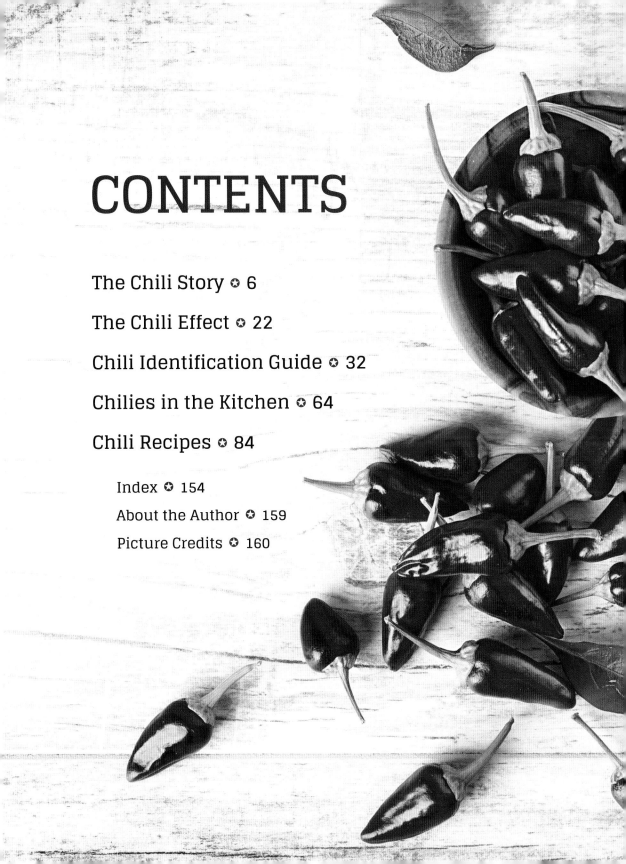

CONTENTS

THE CHILI STORY

This story starts in the jungles of the Amazon, original home of a plant that produces a naturally powerful alkaloid compound. The plant has been spread so diligently that it can now be found on every continent and, although it was virtually unknown outside South America before 1492, it is now common in many parts of the world. On the Indian subcontinent and in the Far East, its use is viewed as indispensable to daily life. In fact, so well has it been accepted there that many assume it is native to the region.

Initially spread by birds, it is humans who took over as the main carriers, developing and spreading the chili as they moved around the planet. Those who come into contact with it report uncontrollable physical symptoms, including sweating, runny noses, and coughing—all of which surprisingly culminate in a general feeling of well-being. Its victims soon feel the need to partake of its delights again, but find they need ever-increasing quantities to regain that initial sensation and satisfy their craving.

A versatile fruit

Chili farming and distribution has become big business, making some individuals both influential and rich. In most countries, you will find devotees growing chilies for their own consumption. They are available in many forms, including fresh, dried, or powdered, as an oleoresin (see page 23), or in the form of a hot sauce. Some varieties are hot- or cold-smoked before use. Many fanatics carry chili products around with them so that they can enjoy their pleasures at any meal, wherever they may be. In their purified state, chilies are used as an effective weapon in close combat, yet they can also provide relief from pain.

Chilies are simple to grow and available everywhere. And although the fruits are capable of causing the most severe discomfort, they have become one of the world's most popular spices.

Right: Red, green, yellow, or purple; long or slender, short or round, twisted or smooth; fresh, dried, raw or cooked—the versatility of chili pods invites experimentation and promises many culinary adventures.

What is a chili?

The genus *Capsicum* is said to have evolved in a corner of South America that is bordered by Bolivia, Brazil, Paraguay, and Argentina. It is here that the greatest number of wild species grow. The chili counts among its family members such species as the potato, tobacco, and even deadly nightshade (*Atropa belladonna*). Along with over 3,000 others, it forms part of the Solanaceae family.

The word "chili" is a legacy of South American civilizations who knew the plants and cultivated different varieties. "Pepper," the confusing alternative, was introduced by Columbus when his voyage took him to South America. So steadfast was he in his belief that he had secured a Spanish trade route to the spices of India that he misnamed the pungent, red chili pods.

Bell peppers and chilies are related, however, and very similar, except that only the chili produces the chemical capsaicin that gives it its pungent taste. So closely related are the two that if you grow chili and pepper varieties in close proximity, they will cross-pollinate. Seeds harvested from peppers that have been crossed will taste hot—in other words, the chili gene will dominate. Plant breeders and seed companies go to great lengths to keep their seed lines pure. Any seeds you procure from a home garden should be viewed with suspicion. You won't know what you get until the plants begin to produce fruit.

Today, chilies and peppers are grown commercially in over 80 countries. The largest harvests come from China, Indonesia, Korea, Mexico, Nigeria, and Turkey—a combined harvesting area not far short of 3,000 square miles (800,000ha). Though mostly grown in warm climes, even the UK has over 247 acres (100ha) of chilies; the U.S. boasts more than 26,000 acres (10,000ha). Production of chilies is booming to satisfy a growing demand.

The chili is often described as "addictive," but not in a negative sense like tobacco, for instance, since no deep craving develops and there is no chemical dependency. It is true, however, that the warming, burning sensation we get from chilies stimulates the release of endorphins—natural painkillers that also create a feeling of well-being. It is therefore quite possible that the enjoyment of chilies is linked to a subconscious desire for this pleasant state of well-being. Sadly, over time, the tolerance to capsaicin increases, meaning we need more or hotter chilies to produce the same sensation.

Left: Nature's Christmas ornaments—chilies not only taste great, they make very attractive ornamental shrubs.

Escape from the jungle

Little is known about chilies before 1492, when Columbus brought the first specimens back to Europe. In her book *Peppers, the Domesticated Capsicums*, Jean Andrews speculates on, and maps out, the probable origin of the species to an area of central Bolivia. It is safe to surmise that the plants originated in the jungles of South America, and that the fruits' fiery taste is an adaptation designed to ward off the attentions of hungry mammals. Birds cannot taste spicy flavors and would not have been affected by this development. For them, the wild chilies were a good source of food, and thus they spread the seeds far and wide.

Evidence for the human use of chilies leads us first to southern Mexico, where archaeologists working in the Tehuacán Valley have found indications that chilies were harvested from wild plants (and may even have been cultivated) as early as 7000 BC. Archaeologist Richard Stockton MacNeish and his team worked from 1960 to 1970 on what became known as the Tehuacán project, during which time they discovered some of the first known evidence of domesticated chilies, maize, squash, tomatoes, and avocados.

In an independent study, a complete pod of the habanero type was found in the Guitarrero cave in Peru. It dates back to 6500 BC and is the earliest known example of this species.

It is believed that Native Americans began to cultivate chili plants between 5200–3400 BC. In Mexico, the Aztecs used chilies to prepare a drink called *chicahuatl*, a thick mixture made of cocoa beans, chilies, corn, and water, that was the ancestor of what we know today as chocolate.

The conquest of Europe

It was from the West Indies that chilies made the leap to Europe. In 1492, Christopher Columbus returned from his second trip to the New World, during which he had attempted to discover a westerly route to the East Indies. King Ferdinand and Queen Isabella of Spain had financed Columbus's expeditions in an attempt to break the Portuguese monopoly over the trade in black pepper, which at the time was worth more than its weight in gold.

Thinking he had reached India, Columbus named the local inhabitants Indians and the chili "pepper," under the misguided assumption that it was related to "black pepper." Columbus, in fact, had discovered the Arawak, who inhabited much of the Caribbean region at the time. They had cultivated the chili, its local name being *ají*, a name still in use today for several varieties.

From Spain, the cultivation of chilies spread across Europe. Gonzálo Percaztegi is believed to have introduced the chili pepper to the Nive Valley in the Basque region of southwestern France in 1523. When the Turks invaded Hungary in 1526, they took along chilies, thus firing the Hungarians' love of paprika. (The invaders themselves had probably been introduced to the chili by Italian or Portuguese traders.) Within a century, the chili had spread to India, Africa, and the Far East along the trade routes frequented by Spanish and Portuguese merchants.

Stories from the New World

As Europeans traveled to Central and South America, they returned with accounts of how the Aztecs and Incas used and worshipped the chili. In 1577, Father Bernardino de Sahagún completed the Florentine Codex, a handwritten encyclopedia of Aztec culture in which he described how chilies were used at almost every meal. In 1609, Garcilaso de la Vega described how the Incas worshipped the chili as Agar-Uchu (Brother Chili Pepper), one of four mythical brothers who featured in the Incan creation story.

The Tabasco™ story

One of the first commercial chili products, this thin, orange-red, slightly sour sauce is still a market leader today. The story of Tabasco™ sauce began in 1865, when Edmund McIlhenny returned home to Avery Island, Louisiana, after the American Civil War. McIlhenny started experimenting with growing what was to become known as the Tabasco chili. How it got this name is not known for certain—there are various scholarly suggestions, each as plausible as the other.

Avery Island was well-suited to growing chilies—in its hot, humid climate, the crops succeeded. Meanwhile, McIlhenny developed the sauce we know today.

In 1868, he formed the McIlhenny Company, which by 1870 had received a patent for its Tabasco-brand sauce. In 1872, an office was opened in England to handle growing demands from Europe. A number of other companies began using the name on their products, and McIlhenny was forced to fight long legal battles, but in 1906 the McIlhenny company registered Tabasco™ as a trademark.

Today, Tabasco™ remains the most successful chili sauce ever made. Although its simple recipe of chili mash, salt, and vinegar has not changed over the years, the bottles have evolved. The brand has been very successfully marketed—despite a number of variant sauces bearing the McIlhenny brand, the original still leads the way.

Right: Ristras of drying chilies decorate a doorway in New Mexico.

Collected and classified

In 1543, the German physician and botanist Leonhard Fuchs illustrated several varieties of chili in *The New Herbal*. From the mid–1700s, chilies entered the scientific mainstream. Swedish-born botanist Carl Linnaeus, one of the founders of the Royal Swedish Academy of Sciences, developed his method of classifying, ranking, and naming living organisms that is still in use today. Linnaeus classified the chili as the genus *Capsicum*. Thanks to him we now distinguish *C. frutescens* (*Capsicum frutescens*) from *C. annuum*, *C. baccatum*, and *C. chinense*.

Using the Linnaean classification method, Philip Miller, botanist and chief gardener at the Chelsea Physic Garden at the time, identified *Capsicum angulofum* in his *The Gardener's and Botanist's Dictionary* in 1768. Unfortunately, the Dutch physician Nikolaus von Jacquin subsequently reclassified the species in 1776 as *Capsicum chinense*. It is not known why he decided on the misnomer *chinense*—he was nowhere near China at the time (collecting plants in the Caribbean for Emperor Francis I of Austria)—but the name has stuck.

In 1794, Spanish botanists Hipolito Ruiz and Joseph Pavon classified *Capsicum pubescens*, the hairy pepper, in their publication *Florae Peruvianae, et Chilensis Podromus*. The two were part of a botanical expedition, sponsored by King Charles III of Spain, that began in 1773 and ended with their return some 11 years later, after almost constant hardship. In his journals, Ruiz described over 2,000 plants and some of their uses.

Carl Linnaeus

Pure capsaicin—the early science of the capsicum

By the 1800s, the art of extracting active ingredients from plants was being perfected. In the case of chilies it was the compounds that gave the pods their heat that were especially sought after. In 1816–17, noted scientists Henri Braconnot and P.A. Bucholz extracted what they called capsicin from a mash of chili peppers and ether, from which the liquid was then filtered and evaporated, leaving a thick reddish substance.

During the 1870s, the scientists Rudolf Buchheim and J.C. Thresh worked independently on the isolation of a pure extract of the pungent compound from the chili pepper. In 1873 Buchheim named his extract capsicol, and just a few years later, in 1876, Thresh isolated a crystalline substance he named capsaicin.

It was not until the 1960s, with the introduction of High-Performance Liquid Chromatography (HPLC), that science discovered that capsaicin was made up not from one, but from a number of discrete compounds; these compounds have been named capsaicinoids. For more information on what makes chilies hot and how the heat is measured, turn to Chapter 2 (page 22).

प्लीज

Chili commerce

Hungary is world famous for its chili powders, which are known universally as paprika. There is an unusual museum dedicated to the history of paprika in the town of Szeged, which, with nearby Kalocsa, vies for the title of paprika capital of Hungary.

The paprika industry was transformed in 1859 when the Palfy brothers of Szeged developed a machine that could control the amount of capsaicin removed from dried chili pods. The machine removed the seeds and veins and then ground the pods into powder, enabling the production of a consistently mild and sweet paprika.

In 1879, the French chef Auguste Escoffier used paprika from Szeged in the kitchens of the Grand Hotel in Monte Carlo. Escoffier's use of what became known as the Hungarian Spice made it indispensable in the foremost kitchens of Europe.

Nowadays, paprika comes in various types, including mild, sweet, rose, and hot, though often it is used simply to add color to a dish. However, good-quality paprika has a subtle and mysteriously bittersweet flavor all its own.

Improving and protecting the stock

Fabian Garcia is a special name in the world of chilies. A professor at New Mexico State University, Garcia produced the first scientifically developed chili in 1894. He aimed to produce a milder fruit that was more acceptable to the general public, with a predictable pungency, size, and shape. The result was the New Mexico No. 9, which, after its introduction in 1913, quickly became the most popular chili among commercial growers in New Mexico, until it was superseded by the New Mexico No. 6 in the 1950s. The No. 6 had the advantage of being only half as hot—at between 700 and 900 Scoville Heat Units (SHU, see page 24)—and producing a higher proportion of well-shaped pods without deep folds in the skin, thus making it easier to process. Before Fabian Garcia, chili production in New Mexico had been a hit-and-miss affair—the quality and the heat of the fruits were very variable. His efforts to create a more consistent harvest turned chili production into a major cash crop for this area.

Left: A chili harvest in India.

Work at New Mexico State University has continued, with Dr. Roy Nakayama and subsequently Dr. Paul Bosland leading the development of commercial chili varieties. With this support, the chili business in New Mexico has grown in value significantly. Only in the last five to ten years has production started to decline as the cost of labor and other factors have favored chilies harvested elsewhere—China, Africa, and India.

The development of chilies at New Mexico State University has produced other notable achievements, including the NuMex Big Jim, which is listed in *The Guinness Book of World Records* as the world's largest chili, its pods growing to lengths of over 7.8" (20cm).

In 1999, *Institut National des Appellations d'Origine* (INAO), the body responsible for the licensing and granting of *Appellation d'Origine Controlée* (AOC) status, moved to protect the unique *Pimente d'Espelette* (Espelette pepper) from imported competition. This protection, also often seen on wines, protects the uniqueness of a product and, at the same time, helps to maintain its quality. Each batch must be presented for approval before it is issued with a number. If specialty regional products are to survive, they will need this kind of protection and control.

The production of the official Espelette pepper is now limited to just 10 communities in the Basque region of southwestern France, near the Spanish border. Since 1967, a chili day has been held in Espelette—an annual celebration of a local harvest that has been grown here since Gonzalo Percaztegi introduced the chili pepper in 1523.

The hottest chili

For years the Red Savina habanero was considered the hottest chili pepper, with its SHU rating of 577,000, but it was unseated in 2007 by the ghost pepper (*naga/bhut jolokia*) at 1,000,000 SHU, which was then unseated in 2013 by the Carolina Reaper (pictured at right) at 2,200,000 SHU, the current holder of the record in *The Guinness Book of World Records*. Still, chili development continues, and a new world's hottest chili could be right around the bend.

Into the future

We are currently in a second boom for chilies. The first was sparked by their discovery and introduction to the West; the second has been encouraged by cheaper traveling costs that enable chili lovers to sample foreign delights and take them back home. We can witness this in supermarkets, which display an increased availability of exotic products due to the growing interest in regional cooking styles. A web search will produce any number of sites with information on how to grow chilies, which has made chili products, previously unheard of outside their native areas, available to a keen world market. Chili festivals are becoming increasingly popular around the world, with annual showcases in the USA, Canada, UK, Australia, France, and South Africa.

The chili has changed from an exotic rarity to a common ingredient in many kitchens. More and more people are enjoying the many varieties that are available, each of which has its own distinctive characteristics.

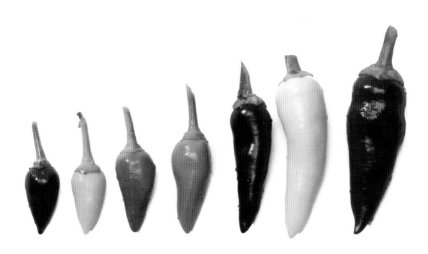

THE CHILI EFFECT

Capsaicin is an alkaloid that has neither flavor nor color and is so robust that it can withstand prolonged periods of drying, freezing, and heating without losing much of its original pungency. When pure capsaicin makes contact with human skin, it causes an excruciating burn, which is why laboratory personnel working with the crystalline alkaloid have to wear full body suits and face masks to prevent accidental contact or inhalation.

The capsaicin found in chilies irritates the pain receptors in the mouth and nose. As soon as the brain receives the pain message, it causes the release of a chemical (substance P) to counteract the condition. Repeated stimulation of the pain receptors leads to a diminished sensitivity, which is why people who regularly eat chilies are far less susceptible to chili burns than those who don't.

It is a fallacy that men can tolerate hotter food than women. The ability to withstand a chili burn has little to do with gender, but depends largely on the distribution of taste buds on the tongue.

Be warned: the consumption of exceptionally hot chilies can cause contact dermatitis. Luckily the damage is hardly permanent—our taste buds are rejuvenated regularly—but if you cannot stand the pain and your mouth is on fire, have a glass of cool milk.

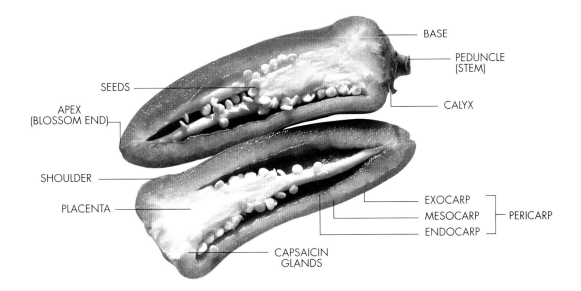

BASE

PEDUNCLE (STEM)

SEEDS

CALYX

APEX (BLOSSOM END)

SHOULDER

EXOCARP
MESOCARP — PERICARP
ENDOCARP

PLACENTA

CAPSAICIN GLANDS

Chili anatomy

Descriptions of chilies tend to use terms that are strange to us. To explain them, above is a picture of a chili, cut and annotated so you can see what is what.

What makes chili hot?

The heat in chilies is produced by chemical compounds called capsaicinoids. These are alkaloid compounds that are produced by glands in the placenta of the fruit. Capsaicinoids are only found in the fruit and are not present in the stems or leaves of the plant. There are a number of different capsaicinoids, the best known of which is capsaicin, which is also the most pungent—in its pure form it is rated at 16,000,000 SHU.

Oleoresin capsicum

If you look at the ingredient lists of some chili sauces, you may come across oleoresin capsicum. This is not a type of plant, but a concentrated form of capsaicinoids extracted from the fruits. Mixing the chili peppers with an organic solvent produces oleoresin capsicum. The resulting liquid is then heated so that the solvent evaporates, leaving behind an oily red mixture containing the capsaicinoids and colorants. Oleoresin can also be made from chilies that have little or no heat, simply to extract their color for use as a food coloring. Manufacturers use oleoresin capsicum to color and flavor products because it provides a controllable level of heat and color in their product. It also has a long shelf life, unlike fresh chilies, which must be processed fairly quickly before they begin to rot.

How hot is hot?

The heat of chili peppers is rated in Scoville Heat Units (SHU), named after Wilbur Scoville, a chemist of the Parke-Davis pharmaceutical company. In 1912, Scoville developed a basic test designed to measure the relative heat of chili pods. Scoville's rather simple method involved a panel of brave tasters and measured the point at which an extract of chili could not be detected in water anymore. His method was unbelievably basic by today's standards: he blended pure ground chilies with sugar water, which was then tasted. The solution was increasingly diluted with sugar water until no heat could be detected. This amount of dilution became the now-famous rating: if the solution consisted of one part extract to 600 parts water, the chili was rated at 600 SHU. As you can guess, the test became increasingly imprecise as the tasters gradually became accustomed to the heat.

Though SHU are still used today to indicate the heat of a chili, the test has now changed to the more scientific and plausible-sounding High-Performance Liquid Chromatography (HPLC), developed in the 1970s for the separation of chemical compounds. Essentially, the technique provides us with a reading of the number—expressed as "parts per million" (ppm)—of compounds present in a solution. As a rough guide to the number of Scoville Heat Units, we would multiply it by 15.

As with most things, the study of chilies is not an exact science—there are many factors that can affect their pungency. For example, hotter chilies tend to come from warmer climates. It has also been proposed that once the fruit is ripening, the heat can be increased by a reduction in watering. For these reasons, chilies are not given a single-value Scoville rating, but are normally sold with two values, showing the minimum and maximum values you can expect from the variety, as illustrated on page 27 (see also Chapter 3, starting on page 32).

How to cure a chili burn

Capsaicin affects the pain receptors in the mouth, nerves that normally sense heat. Since capsaicinoids, the constituent components of capsaicin, are not water-soluble, water will quench a chili burn only temporarily. At worst it may increase it, because water simply serves to wash the capsaicinoids around the mouth. Various remedies have been suggested, but none can cure a chili burn instantly because of the localized effect of capsaicin on the pain receptors in the mouth.

If you are really desperate, have a glass of milk or eat some yogurt, ice cream, or a slice of bread with a thick layer of butter. The fats and oils in these foods will quickly absorb the burn.

You could also consider downing a cool beer. Though it cannot really reduce the heat in your mouth, it does numb the rest of the body.

Chili-based dishes are often served with rice or breads; while not as effective as oils at reducing the burn, they do help to soak up the capsaicinoids and clean the mouth. With continued exposure you will become more tolerant to capsaicinoids and will be able to taste food again. Unfortunately, capsaicinoids are not broken down by the digestive system. Some experts recommend bananas to soothe any internal/external discomfort, but the best prevention lies in moderate consumption.

Right: Bell peppers have a zero SHU rating and are delicious in salads.

Pepper/chili	Scoville units (SHU)
bell pepper	0
poblano	1,000–2,000
jalapeño	2,000–5,000
serrano	8,000–20,000
de árbol	15,000–30,000
Tabasco	30,000–50,000
habanero	200,000–300,000
ghost pepper	800,000–1,000,000
Carolina Reaper	1,600,000–2,200,000
pure capsaicin	16,000,000

The medical uses of capsicum

Herbalist Dr. John R. Christopher, an advocate of the medicinal properties of capsicum, used cayenne in many of his preparations and wrote several books about its use and benefits. Still available is the 600-page shopper called *The School of Natural Healing: The Reference Volume on Natural Herbs for the Teacher, Student, or Herbal Practitioner*, which was his major work on the subject.

If Columbus and his crew had eaten some of the chilies they discovered on their journey, they would not have suffered from scurvy. This is because chilies are rich in vitamin C. The US Department of Agriculture's National Nutrient Database lists red peppers as being endowed with 143.7mg of vitamin C per 100g, while oranges contain only 4w5mg per 100g. Vitamin C is an antioxidant used by the body to soak up free radicals. Chilies also contain other antioxidants: lutein is found in red chilies, while alpha-carotene is found in yellow and orange chilies as well as peppers.

Over the years, a growing number of commercial products has included the ingredient capsaicin to relieve various aches and pains. Probably one of the very oldest is Sloan's Liniment Rub, originally developed for veterinary use, which was manufactured from 1903 by Dr. Earl S. Sloan, Inc. The product contains oleoresin capsicum to produce a localized heat effect that causes increased blood flow and results in reddened skin. It was recommended for the relief of rheumatism and muscular soreness. Sloan's Liniment Rub is still available today, though these days Pfizer owns the brand. A German company produces a capsicum plaster that claims to be a "remedy for lumbago," offering relief from pain, stiff muscles, and cramps. Various other products use capsicum to similar effect, while others are designed to alleviate shingles, diabetic neuropathy, and various other painful ailments.

Apart from claiming to be able to alleviate various physical conditions, chili is also known to affect our mood. Capsicum causes the brain to release endorphins, natural painkillers that produce a feeling of well-being.

Left: A poblano ancho chili.

Pepper sprays—non-lethal defense

Chilies have found a use in self-defense, and capsicum sprays are used around the world as a defense against animals. (The US Postal Service issues a spray to postal carriers to protect them from dog attacks; the spray's ingredients are modelled on the potent chemical makeup of chilies.) Originally developed in the 1960s by Professor James Jenkins and Dr. Frank Hayes at Georgia State University, pepper spray was initially marketed as "Halt Animal Repellent."

Extra-high-potency versions have been developed to protect even against bear attacks, while milder versions are marketed as personal defense sprays. But these have now been declared illegal in many countries. Pepper spray causes swelling of the mucous membranes, an involuntary closing of the eyes and copious tearing, coughing, and irritation and severe inflammation of the respiratory tract.

The spray is made from oleoresin capsicum, which is mixed with alcohol or another organic solvent that acts as a carrier. Pressurized gas is used as propellant. In 1989, the FBI published a report on the effects of pepper sprays: after three years of study and testing on over 800 willing subjects, the investigators reported no lasting medical effects, which led to the use of capsicum sprays by law enforcement agencies around the world.

The campaign against the use of such sprays has been vigorous, and the debate continues: in 1997, Amnesty International condemned the US police in California for their use of pepper spray against peaceful protesters, calling it "tantamount to torture."

In the UK, it is illegal to possess pepper sprays, even for self-defense, and there is currently a worldwide ban on bringing them aboard aircraft. In the USA, laws vary widely from state to state and city to city.

Other uses

There are over 1,200 patented products that include capsicum or chili peppers. These include insecticide, a spray to inhibit web growth and discourage spiders, a boat anti-fouling coating, pain relievers, and disinfectants.

Left: Chilies are often dried spread out on the floor, as here in Stonetown, Zanzibar.

CHILI IDENTIFICATION GUIDE

Before we take a look at some chili varieties, let me explain a little about their family tree. Chilies belong to the Solanaceae family, which has over 3,000 members. Within this family, chilies come from the genus *Capsicum*, which includes five domesticated species and at least another 20 known wild ones. Each species is again subdivided into varieties. On the labels in garden centers and on seed packets, you will see the varieties classified as follows: *C. chinense* red habanero. The *C.* is for the genus, *Capsicum*, while *chinense* denotes the species, and red habanero the variety.

There are thousands of varieties, and more are developed all the time by universities and commercial companies around the world. Food companies are always looking for a more consistently shaped pod to make processing simpler, or a lower-heat jalapeño to make Tex-Mex dishes more palatable to a wider market. In some countries plant breeders can apply for PVR (Plant Variety Rights), which gives them some protection and allows them to control the commercialization of varieties they have developed.

Right: Chilies come in a multitude of shapes, sizes, and colors—usually, the more attractive they are to look at, the hotter they are, so handle with care and experiment with caution.

The five domesticated species

TABASCO
C. frutescens

SCOTCH BONNET
C. chinense

JALAPEÑO
C. annuum

MANZANO
C. pubescens

C. frutescens

These have two or more purple or greenish white flowers at each node.
Examples: Tabasco chili, bird pepper, japóne.

C. chinense

This species, which produces some of the very hottest varieties, was incorrectly named by the Dutch physician Nikolaus von Jacquin in 1776, who thought it came from China.
Examples: habanero, Scotch bonnet.

C. annuum

This, the most commonly cultivated chili, has hundreds—if not thousands—of varieties.
Examples: poblano, Anaheim, jalapeño, Peter Pepper, Cayenne, bird's-eye (Thai), pasilla.

C. pubescens

Named for the fine hairs that cover the underside of its leaves and stems, these chilies' seeds are black and cannot be cross-pollinated with any of the other species. This limitation has probably kept the number of varieties of this species much lower than the rest. One of the most hardy species, the plants have been grown at higher altitudes and can withstand much lower temperatures, even light frost.
Examples: manzano.

CRIOLLA SELLA
C. baccatum

C. baccatum

The name *baccatum* refers to the small, berry-like fruit that is characteristic of wild chili species. The varieties we are seeing today, however, are the result of centuries of careful cultivation and selective breeding.
Examples: ají amarillo, Brazilian starfish.

Describing capsicum plants and fruits

The booklet published in 1995 by the International Plant Genetic Resources Institute (IPGRI) provides excellent descriptions of the growing conditions of capsicum plants, as well as the shape of their leaves, the positions of flowers, and the shapes and colors of the fruit. This last point is especially interesting, as it is what most of us are ever likely to see of the plant. If seed and plant merchants were to employ such a detailed method of description, much confusion would be avoided, and it would certainly help with identification.

A disclaimer about heat ratings

All of the SHU ratings given in this guide are estimated values, providing an indication of the expected heat level for the chili. Many chilies have never been officially tested for their SHU rating. You should also be aware that often seeds of one chili variety are sold under incorrect names (unwittingly or intentionally); sometimes the variety being sold isn't even close to the label on the package. Because many seeds look alike, it's difficult to be sure what you're buying, so purchase from a reputable source whenever possible.

Chili identification guide

This guide presents the varieties you are most likely to come across, both fresh and dried. Familiarize yourself with their names—many chilies look so similar that trying to identify them by their fruit alone is a fool's mission. Scoville Heat Units are indicated where they are available and were correct at the time of going to print; the color bar below each reading is an artistic representation of the pungency.

Ají Amarillo

Also variously known as yellow *ají*, *ají verde*, *ají fresco*, and *ají escabeche*, these thin-fleshed Andean chilies ripen from yellow to orange. They grow to 3.9" (10cm) long and 1–1.5" (3–4cm) in diameter, tapering to a point, and are often sold dried or as a powder. They are rarely found outside South America.
Species: *C. baccatum*
SHU: 40,000–50,000

Ají Cereza

The cereza, whose name means cherry in Spanish, grows wild in the Peruvian rainforests and attains a width of about 0.7–1" (2–3 cm).
Species: *C. annuum*
SHU: 70,000–80,000

Ají Dulce

Dulce means sweet, and this is indeed a no-heat habanero. "And what use is that?" I hear you cry. Wouldn't it be great to know what chilies really taste like before the heat kicks in? Well, here's your chance—and if that doesn't appeal, why not impress your friends in the pub by eating this habanero whole in front of them without flinching? The fruits grow to 1–2" (3–5cm) long and 0.9–1.3" (2.5–3.5cm) in diameter, maturing from green through orange to red when fully ripe. Be careful though: the seed can pick up the hot habit if it is crossbred with a more potent variety.
Species: *C. chinense*
SHU: 1,000

Ají Limo
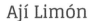

The fruit of this small Peruvian variety grows 1.5–2" (4–5cm) long and 0.7–1" (2–3cm) in diameter, starting at a very pale yellow and maturing through purple, yellow, and orange to red.
Species: *C. chinense*
SHU: 50,000–60,000

Ají Limón

The fruits of this Peruvian chili grow 1.5–2.7" (4–7cm) long and up to 0.7" (2cm) in diameter. They start as a greenish yellow and turn lemon yellow when fully ripe. Their thin flesh makes them ideal for drying, and they add an interesting touch of color when added to a string of chilies to form ristras (decorative garlands of dried chilies).
Species: *C. baccatum*
SHU: 40,000–60,000

Ají Pinguita de Mono

Popular all over Peru but rarely available outside the country, these chilies are not grown commercially. The small fruits grow to between 0.6–0.9" (1.5–2.5cm) long and mature to a deep red.
Species: *C. annuum*
SHU: 70,000–80,000

Ammazzo

This is a very unusual looking Italian chili whose fruits cluster together on the ends of branches in bunches of 8–15. The fruits grow to between 0.4–0.7" (1–2cm) in diameter, maturing from bottle green to red and very similar in appearance to the nosegay chili, which also produces bunches of ripe red fruits.
Species: *C. annuum*
SHU: 1,500–5,000

Anaheim

This mild green chili is named after the Southern California city. The long fruits grow to between 5.8–7.8" (15–20cm) and are ideal for stuffing (*chiles rellenos*), grilling, or pickling. They are mostly used when green (thus the low heat rating here), but become hotter when fully ripened to red. Anaheims have a tough outer skin that can be removed by roasting and peeling (see Chapter 4, page 64). They are available both dried and fresh from specialty retailers or by mail order.
Species: *C. annuum*
SHU: 1,000–10,000

Ancho

The ancho is a dried poblano. It is normally smaller and lighter in color than the *mulato*. Together with the pasilla and *mulato*, it forms part of the trinity of chilies used in the Mexican national dish *mole*. Anchos should be rehydrated in warm water for 15–20 minutes before use.
Species: *C. annuum*
SHU: 1,000–2,000

Antohi Romanian

This sweet pepper, originally from Romania, is now popular in the USA. The story goes that the seeds arrived with defecting acrobat Jan Antohi in 1991. The fruits grow to 3.9" (10cm) in length and up to 2" (5cm) in diameter. When ripe they are red, starting from yellow through orange.
Species: *C. annuum*
SHU: 0

Apache F1

This dwarf hybrid chili makes an ideal pot plant and can be displayed on the patio during the warm summer months in the northern hemisphere. It produces a good crop of fruits, 2–2.7" (5–7cm) long and 0.6–0.9" (1.5–2.5cm) in diameter at the shoulder, that turn red when ripe. Unlike some other highly developed varieties, it keeps a good grip on its fruits, which can be left on the plant until needed.
Species: *C. annuum*
SHU: 70,000–80,000

Bacio di Satana

The "kiss of the devil"—a small, cherry-shaped chili, 0.7–1" (2–3cm) in diameter—comes from Italy. The fruits ripen from green to red. Their thick walls make them ideal for stuffing; they are delicious stuffed with cheese and then baked or grilled in the oven.

Species: *C. annuum*
SHU: 40,000–50,000

Bangalore Torpedo

Growing to 23.5" (60cm) high, this Indian shrub produces long and twisted fruits that are 3.9–5.4" (10–14cm) long and 0.4–0.7" (1–2cm) in diameter at the shoulder. The fruits ripen from lime green to red, are good for pickling whole, and are easy to dry.

Species: *C. frutescens*
SHU: 15,000–25,000

Bird's-eye

This variety, whose diminutive size hides a searing heat, is also known as Thai or tiny chili. It can be found in most good Asian supermarkets, it is simple to grow at home, and it is not uncommon to get hundreds of fruits from a single plant.

Species: *C. annuum*
SHU: 100,000–175,000

Boldog

This genuine variety of Hungarian paprika produces smooth fruits that grow to between 3.9–5.8" (10–15cm) long and 0.7–1.5" (2–4cm) in diameter. They are the best choice for making your own paprika, as the thin walls make them very easy to dry. For the best results, remove the seeds and placenta before drying.

Species: *C. annuum*
SHU: 0–100

Brazilian Starfish

The unusual, flattened fruits that grow to only 0.7–1" (2–3cm) high but 1–1.5" (3–4cm) in diameter, with vertical ribs, look like short-tentacled starfish when viewed from above, hence the name. The fruits mature from green to bright red. This is a very interesting looking variety and makes an attractive ornamental plant.
Species: *C. baccatum*
SHU: 10,000–30,000

Bulgarian Carrot

The stocky plants remain under 23.5" (60cm) in height and yield an impressive harvest that resembles small carrots, so it is not difficult to imagine how this variety got its name. A fast-ripening variety, it likes full sun, and the thin-skinned fruits, 2.7–3.9" (7–10cm) long, are good in salsas and chutneys.
Species: *C. annuum*
SHU: 10,000–30,000

Capónes

Capónes are red jalapeños whose seeds were removed before smoking. The deseeding process is very laborious, which makes capónes quite expensive and means that they are not widely available.
Species: *C. annuum*
SHU: 5,000–8,000

Carolina Reaper

This chili broke the record for hottest chili in 2013 and then broke it again in 2017 with an even higher SHU rating. Developed by Ed Currie of the PuckerButt Pepper Company in South Carolina, it's not for the faint of heart. The company is currently at work testing the heat of one of their new chili varieties, Pepper X, that may very well unseat the Carolina Reaper.
Species: *C. chinense*
SHU: 1,600,000–2,200,000

Casabella

This is a red or yellow, thin-walled chili that grows up to 1.5" (4cm) long. It has a low to medium heat and is good in stews and salsas.
Species: *C. annuum*
SHU: 1,500–4,000

Cascabel

The *bola* (Spanish for ball) chili, which is known in its dried form as *cascabel* (Spanish for rattle), is a dark reddish brown fruit some 0.7–1.5" (2–4cm) in diameter. It probably gets its name from the way the seeds rattle inside the dried fruit. It can be used in sauces, salsas, stews, and soups.
Species: *C. annuum*
SHU: 1,000–2,500

Cayenne

There seem to be almost any number of cayenne varieties that range from miniatures to some that are almost 7.8" (20cm) long. The fruit is thin and tapers to a sharp point. Popular in Indian and Chinese dishes, cayenne pepper have also been used in medical research: the fruits contain, among other things, anticoagulants that help to stop blood from clotting. It is also claimed that they increase the metabolic rate.
Species: *C. annuum*
SHU: 30,000–50,000

Charleston Hot

Related to the cayenne, but much hotter, the Charleston Hot yields thick-walled, straight or slightly curved fruits up to 3.9" (10cm) in length and 0.7" (2cm) in diameter, ripening from green to yellow, then bright orange. Released in 1974 at Clemson University, South Carolina, this variety was developed to resist root knot nematodes. It is said that the peppers "rival the heat of Charleston in August." They are popular with gardeners but can be hard to germinate, as they need temperatures around 78.8°F (26°C) for a few weeks.
Species: *C. annuum*
SHU: 80,000–100,000

Cherry Bomb F1

The Cherry Bomb F1 is a good example of an early-yielding, small, and compact chili plant. The fruits grow up to 2.7" (7cm) in diameter and ripen from green to bright red.
Species: *C. annuum*
SHU: 2,500–5,000

Chi-Chen

The *chi-chen* produces bright red, thin-walled, very hot fruits, growing up to 2.7" (7cm) long and 0.4–0.6" (1–1.5cm) in diameter. Ideal in Chinese or Thai cuisine, they also make excellent ornamental plants. The fruits are easily dried and the thin skins become almost translucent.
Species: *C. annuum*
SHU: 60,000–70,000

Chilhuacle Amarillo

Chilhuacle amarillo (yellow), also known as *chilaca* (the fresh form of the pasilla), hails from the Oaxaca and Chiapas regions of Mexico. The reddish yellow fruits, 2.3–3.1" (6–8cm) long and 1–2" (3–5cm) in diameter with broad shoulders, are used in *moles*, to which they impart a strong yellow color. Available outside Mexico in dried form, generally only from specialty stores, they are worth hunting down for their excellent, slightly sweet acidic flavor.
Species: *C. annuum*
SHU: 4,000–8,000

Chilhuacle Negro

Chilhuacle negro (black) produces fruits that are heart-shaped like bell peppers, 2–3.1" (5–8cm) long and the same across the shoulders, shiny and an attractive, dark mahogany color. They have a wonderful, dark liquorice flavor, and are used to make black *mole*—a speciality of southwestern Mexico. Outside Mexico they can be found dried at specialty retailers.
Species: *C. annuum*
SHU: 2,500–3,500

Chilhuacle Rojo

Chilhuacle rojo (red) also hails from southwestern Mexico. The fruits are dark red in color and grow 2.3–3.1" (6–8cm) long and 0.7–1.5" (2–4cm) in diameter at the shoulders. This chili is another staple of the Mexican national dish, *mole*. Outside Mexico, it can be found dried at specialty Mexican retailers.
Species: *C. annuum*
SHU: 1,000–2,000

Chimayó

This fast-maturing variety is named after a town in New Mexico. The large, thick-fleshed chilies are similar to the Anaheim variety, but hotter, and grow to 7.8" (20cm) long. They mature to red and can often be found dried and powdered in specialty stores. Like the Anaheim, the Chimayó is picked when it is green and used in stews, in salsas, or stuffed (*chiles rellenos*).
Species: *C. annuum*
SHU: 4,000–6,000

Chipotle

The chipotle is not a variety at all, but is becoming the generic term for any smoked chili. Ripe red jalapeños are most commonly preserved by smoking and drying. This is traditionally done in the field: chilies are placed on racks in a large pit, or smoke hut, and smoke from a nearby fire pit is channeled past the fruits. The fire, kept well-controlled and starved of oxygen, produces the smoke required to gradually dry the chilies. The versatile chipotle is used in many dishes because it imparts a wonderful smoky flavor with the characteristic mild heat of the jalapeño.
Species: *C. annuum*
SHU: 5,000–8,000

Choricero

This sweet, mild chili from Spain, often found dried or as a paste, grows to 2.7–3.5" (7–9cm) long and 1.5–2.3" (4–6cm) in diameter, ripening from green to red. *Choriceros* are used to flavor the spicy *chorizo* sausage, as well as traditional rice dishes such as *paella*.
Species: *C. annuum*
SHU: 0

Christmas Bell

This unusual Dutch chili variety is uniquely shaped like a Christmas tree ornament. At between 2–2.7" (5–7cm) long and the same in diameter, the fruits are first green and then bright red when fully ripe. Use them in salsa and summer salads.

Species: *C. baccatum*
SHU: 5,000–15,000

Costeño Amarillo

One of the few yellow chilies grown in Mexico comes from the states of Oaxaca, Veracruz, and Guerrero. They are often used in *mole amarillo* (yellow *mole*). The thin-fleshed fruits grow 2.3–2.7" (6–7cm) long and up to 0.7" (2cm) in diameter at the shoulders, tapering to a point.

Species: *C. annuum*
SHU: 1,200–2,000

Criolla Sella

This Bolivian chili produces cylindrical fruits 2–3.1" (5–8cm) long and 0.4–0.7" (1–2cm) in diameter that ripen from green to orange when fully mature. The thin flesh makes them simple to dry, but the *criolla sella* is also good for adding to salsas or salads.

Species: *C. baccatum*
SHU: 25,000–30,000

Cyklon

This variety of chili is used to make dark-red paprika and comes from Poland. The fruits grow 3.5–4.2" (9–11cm) long and 0.9–1.3" (2.5–3.5cm) in diameter at the shoulder, tapering to a point. Mature fruits are thin-fleshed, hot, and easy to dry. The best paprika is made after removing the seeds and placenta.

Species: *C. annuum*
SHU: 1,000–5,000

Dagger Pod

With its long, slender pod and gentle curve, it takes little imagination to see this chili's resemblance to the sheath for a *kukri*, the short knife once used by Gurkha soldiers. The fruits grow to between 3.9–5.4" (10–14cm) long and 0.4–0.7" (1–2cm) in diameter, maturing from green through orange to red when ripe. They are good in stews.
Species: *C. frutescens*
SHU: 30,000–50,000

Datil

From St. Augustine in Florida comes the datil, a habanero-style chili that is popular with the local Minorcan community, with whom it arrived in 1777 when they abandoned the slave-like conditions in the New Smyrna settlement. The datil is a prolific producer of dark yellow or orange fruits that grow to between 2–3.1" (5–8cm) long and up to 0.7" (2cm) in diameter. Like habaneros, they are very hot.
Species: *C. chinense*
SHU: 200,000–300,000

De Árbol

The *de árbol* is so named because the bush resembles a small tree. It is related to the cayenne and is also known as bird's beak. The fruits are 2–3.9" (5–10cm) long and deep red in color. The thin flesh is easy to dry and often used to spice oils and vinegars.
Species: *C. annuum*
SHU: 15,000–30,000

Facing-Heaven

From the Sichuan province of China comes the Facing-Heaven chili, also known as *Chi Ying Jiao*, so-called because its bright red conical fruits, which grow 3.1–3.9" (8–10cm) long, point to the sky. These chilies can be found in good Asian supermarkets.
Species: *C. chinense*
SHU: 30,000–50,000

Fataali

10

The dangerous sounding *fataali* is a habanero relative from central Africa. The wrinkled fruits start green, maturing to bright yellow. They grow to between 2.3–3.5" (6–9cm) long and 1–1.5" (3–4cm) in diameter at the shoulder, tapering to a point. Like habaneros, these chilies are fiery hot and should be handled with care.
Species: *C. chinense*
SHU: 100,000–300,000

Filius Blue

8

A compact ornamental chili with purple to almost blue leaves, the small egg-shaped fruits are first purple and eventually ripen to red. This variety is not noted for its flavor but is very good for adding heat.
Species: *C. annuum*
SHU: 30,000–50,000

Ornamental Firecracker

9

Not to be confused with the Indian hybrid firecracker (below), the ornamental firecracker produces many small upright conical fruits, 0.4–1" (1–3cm) long, that ripen from purple to orange and red. Like other ornamental plants, this provides a most impressive display.
Species: *C. annuum*
SHU: 50,000–100,000

Firecracker

8

This compact plant produces a mass of cone-shaped fruits, 0.4–0.7" (1–2cm) long and around 0.4–0.6" (1–1.5 cm) in diameter, that ripen from white through purple to orange and finally red. This makes for a very showy display, but be careful: the fruit lives up to its name and is very hot.
Species: *C. annuum*
SHU: 30,000–50,000

Fish

This chili has variegated leaves and fruits that are green with yellow or white stripes and mature through orange to red. This variety is of African-American heritage, rare and unique. The chilies are popular in shellfish dishes.
Species: *C. annuum*
SHU: 5,000–25,000

Fresno

Named after the town in California, the Fresno is easily confused with jalapeño or serrano chilies. The 2–3.1" (5–8cm) long conical fruits are milder when green, ripening to red, and often used in salsa. A waxy skin and thick flesh makes them difficult to dry, so they are best preserved by pickling or freezing.
Species: *C. annuum*
SHU: 3,000–8,000

Garden Salsa F1

Bred for flavor, not heat, this is a very versatile chili, good in salsas and sauces. Its size, 7–8.6" (18–22cm) long and 1–2" (3–5cm) in diameter, makes the fruits good for stuffing, or for cutting into strips to be fried. The fruits ripen to red but are most often used when green, and they are best roasted to remove the skin. To get a decent crop, the plants need to be grown in a sunny location.
Species: *C. annuum*
SHU: 2,000–4,500

Georgia Flame

Deep red, thick-walled, and crunchy, these fruits grow up to 5.9" (15cm) long and 2–2.3" (5–6cm) at the shoulder; they are good for producing hot salsa, for stuffing, and for baking. This variety comes from the Republic of Georgia.
Species: *C. annuum*
SHU: 1,500

Goat's Horn

This versatile variety originated in Asia. It is a hot chili that produces lots of twisted, glossy fruits—green maturing to red—up to 5.4" (14cm) long and 1" (3cm) in diameter.
Species: *C. annuum*
SHU: 1,500–2,500

Guindilla

Outside Spain this popular chili is most often found dried and strung up in ristras. The fruit is thin-fleshed, grows to between 2.7–4.6" (7–12cm) long and 0.4–0.7" (1–2cm) in diameter, and is used for its excellent flavor. In Spain they are often used for tapas (light snacks or appetizers) when they are still green, the green pod not having acquired the pungency of the fully ripe version.
Species: *C. annuum*
SHU: 1,000–2,000

Habanero 10

After the jalapeño, this chili, whose name means "from Havana," is probably the best-known variety, its famed heat making it a favorite. They are grown extensively in the Yucatán Peninsula of Mexico and in Belize, where Marie Sharp's hot sauce is made. The fruits have a very attractive Chinese lantern shape and can grow to 2–2.3" (5–6cm) long and 0.7–1" (2–3cm) in diameter. The most common varieties produce green fruits that ripen to orange. Habaneros need to be handled with some care. They are extremely hot and can easily cause blisters on the skin and tongue. Use them very sparingly and wear gloves when you are handling the fruits.

They are best grown in warm or tropical climates, take a long time to germinate, and are considered the "hothouse flower" of the chili world. The plants require a lot of sunlight if the fruits are to ripen fully, so they cannot be recommended for growers in the northern hemisphere. The variety is grown mainly as an annual, as it does not winter well.

Common varieties include red, brown, chocolate-brown, and orange habaneros. See also Habanero Red Savina, datil, paper lantern habanero, Scotch bonnet, fataali, and *naga/bhut jolokia*.
Species: *C. chinense*
SHU: 200,000–300,000

Habanero Red Savina

Red Savina is probably the ultimate in habanero-style chilies. In 1994, it recorded an amazing 577,000 SHU. Few come hotter than this. The fruits grow up to 2" (5cm) long and 1–1.5" (3–4cm) in diameter. Developed after a lucky find by Frank Garcia of GNS Spices, it is much prized by sauce makers. The seeds are protected by Plant Variety Protection 9200255 and are only sold to home gardeners for their own use. Seeds from the crops must not be sold. The seeds can take a long time to germinate, so be patient. In cooking it must be treated with great care—just a few grams in a meal can be overpowering. You have been warned!
Species: *C. chinense*
SHU: 350,000–577,000

Hungarian Yellow Wax Hot

The fruits of this variety, which is also known as banana pepper, ripen to an orange-red but are harvested yellow, as this is when the flavor is best. The crisp flesh is ideal for use in salads and salsas. The fruits grow to 4.6–5.4" (12–14cm) long and up to 1.5" (4cm) in diameter.
Species: *C. annuum*
SHU: 2,000–4,000

Inferno F1

This Hungarian Wax hybrid produces masses of thick-walled pendant fruits, 7–7.8" (18–20cm) long and 1–1.5" (3–4cm) in diameter. They start a greenish yellow and ripen to red, have an exceptional flavor, and are good in many dishes.
Species: *C. annuum*
SHU: 2,500–4,000

Jalapeño   5

This is probably the best-known chili in the world and has
many different varieties, from the Tam Mild developed at Texas
A&M University, to the Gigantia, which can grow to longer than
4.6" (12cm). In America, an industry has developed around this chili,
from growing and processing to selling, design, and sales of equipment
for the home gardener. The Campbell Soup Company even holds a US
patent for a "no-heat jalapeño."

The jalapeño normally grows between 2–3.9" (5–10cm) long and
1–1.5" (3–4cm) in diameter with a very distinctive cylindrical shape.
It is most often eaten green, but can also be used when a fully mature
red. The fruit is often found with "corking" lines (like white stretch
marks) on the skin, but don't let this put you off—these are the best
ones. The sweet heat from these fleshy chilies has made them popular
around the world. Jalapeños are the staple of Tex-Mex cuisine, where
they can be found on nachos, stuffed with cheese and coated in bread
crumbs, or used in sauces and almost everything else that can be done
with a chili. Ripe red jalapeños that have been smoked are known as
chipotles—this is a traditional Mexican method of preserving the crop.

Common varieties include Gigantia (an extra-large variety), Early
(early fruiting variety), Tam Mild (smaller with less heat), and Sweet.
Species: *C. annuum*
SHU: 2,000–5,000

Jaloro   8

Developed and released in 1992 at Texas A&M University by plant
virologist and breeder Ben Villalon, this is a uniquely yellow jalapeño.
It was developed to be resistant to viruses but still provides all the heat
of its ancestor. It matures from yellow to red, but like the jalapeño is
customarily used when it is still yellow and not fully ripe.
Species: *C. annuum*
SHU: 30,000–50,000

Jamaican Hot Chocolate

Another very hot relative of the habanero and Scotch bonnet, the Jamaican Hot Chocolate is believed to have originated from fruits discovered in the market in Port Antonio, Jamaica. When ripe, these chilies are chocolate brown, about 1.5–2.3" (4–6cm) long and 1–1.5" (3–4cm) in diameter, with deep ribs and a wrinkled skin.
Species: *C. chinense*
SHU: 100,000–200,000

Japóne

Used in Chinese, Thai, and Japanese dishes, japónes are red dried peppers, 1–3.5" (3–9cm) long and 0.4–0.7" (1–2cm) in diameter. They are similar to the *de árbol* and can be used in sauces and stir-fries.
Species: *C. frutescens*
SHU: 20,000–25,000

Joe's Long

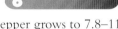

This extremely long, red cayenne pepper grows to 7.8–11.7" (20–30cm) but is only around 0.6" (1.5cm) in diameter. Thin-walled, it dries well but is ideally used fresh in Thai cooking or for pickling whole in (long) jars.
Species: *C. annuum*
SHU: 20,000

Jwala

From India comes the jwala, a prolific variety that produces many thin green pods, 3.9" (10cm) long and 0.4–0.7" (1–2cm) in diameter. They are often pickled green but mature to a deep red. Easy to grow, the plants are also quite attractive and can be likened to an umbrella because the fruits hang down below a canopy of leaves.
Species: *C. annuum*
SHU: 20,000–30,000

Kashmiri Degi Mirch

From Kashmir, the northernmost state of India, comes the degi mirch. It is rare outside India, as demand far outstrips supply; as a result, other chilies are frequently passed off as the real thing.

About 2" (5cm) long and 0.7" (2cm) in diameter, the real degi mirch is a deep crimson, thin-walled fruit most often found dried or in powder form in Indian markets. Although not a very hot chili, its sweet flavor makes it wonderful in milder dishes.

Species: *C. annuum*
SHU: 1,000–2,000

Manzano

This chili, also known as *manzana, rocoto, locoto, canario, caballo,* and *perón,* is one of the few South American varieties not of the *C. annuum* species. The fruits have large, dark brown to black seeds and small hairs on their leaves and stems—all features unique to *C. pubescens.* Shaped like a small apple (*manzana*), each fruit is 0.7–1" (2–3cm) in diameter with thick flesh, initially green and ripening to yellow, orange, and red, depending on the variety. The plants are more resistant to lower temperatures than other species and are therefore ideal for cooler climates, but still require protection from frost.

Species: *C. pubescens*
SHU: 30,000–50,000

Mirasol (Miracielo)

This variety was named *mirasol* (looking at the sun), possibly because the pointed fruits grow erect. When dried the chili is known as a *guajillo,* sometimes also called *travieso* (mischievous). The fruits ripen to dark red and reach about 4.6–6.2" (12–16cm) in length and 1–2" (3–5cm) in diameter. When dried they have an exceptionally tough skin and need long soaking before use. Less sweet, but a little hotter than the ancho, they are used in similar recipes—commonly in *chilaquile* (a casserole of tortillas, spicy tomatoes, and cheese).

Species: *C. annuum*
SHU: 2,500–4,000

Mulato

The *mulato* is a dried poblano and is generally larger and darker in color than the ancho. Together with the pasilla and ancho, it makes up the trinity of chilies used in the Mexican national dish, *mole*. Rehydrate the dried fruits in warm water for 15–20 minutes before use.
Species: *C. annuum*
SHU: 2,500–3,000

Naga/Bhut Jolokia (Ghost Pepper)

In 2000, this variety from Assam, India, was touted as the world's hottest chili, rumored to have beaten the previous record holder, the Red Savina, with a rating of 855,000 SHU. It wasn't until 2007 that a verified rating of 1,000,000 SHU was officially recorded, and the chili was also reclassified from *C. frutescens* to *C. chinense*. The most common name people know this chili by is ghost pepper. It was considered the hottest chili in the world until it was unseated by the Carolina Reaper in 2013.
Species: *C. chinense*
SHU: 855,000–1,000,000

New Mexico No. 9

This, the first scientifically developed chili, was created by Fabian Garcia of New Mexico State University and released in 1913. Its predictable pungency, as well as shape and size, soon made it the favorite with commercial growers in the area.
Species: *C. annuum*
SHU: 1,000–5,000

New Mexico Sandia

Another chili produced by the prolific New Mexico State University, this one developed by Dr. Roy Harper and released in 1956, the Sandia is a cross between the original New Mexico No. 9 and an Anaheim-type chili. It produces long, straight fruits 5.9–7" (15–18cm) long by 1–2" (3–5cm) in diameter at the shoulder that ripen from dark green to bright red. They have less severe folds in the skin than Anaheims and have a flattened body.
Species: *C. annuum*
SHU: 1,000–2,500

NuMex Big Jim

The world's largest chili pepper, growing up to 11.7" (30cm) long, was developed by Dr. Nakayama at New Mexico State University in 1975. Big Jim produces long, thick, fleshy fruits. Developed for commercial production, it is also a popular chili to grow at home, as it yields an impressive crop.
Species: *C. annuum*
SHU: 500–1,000

NuMex Twilight

Developed by Paul Bosland and Jaime Iglesias in 1994 at the New Mexico State University, this ornamental plant produces purple fruits that develop through yellow to red when ripe. This is a compact variety commonly grown in pots that produces an impressive display of fruits.
Species: *C. annuum*
SHU: 30,000–50,000

Orozco

The Orozco hails from Eastern Europe and produces large fruits up to 3.9" (10cm) long and 2" (5cm) in diameter, maturing from green to bright orange. Like some other Eastern European varieties, its fruits resemble carrots.
Species: *C. annuum*
SHU: 20,000–30,000

Paper Lantern Habanero

10

Unusually shaped for a habanero, the pointed, elongated fruits of this variety ripen from lime green through orange to bright red. This plant is ideal for colder climates, where other habanero varieties can only produce a disappointing crop.

Species: *C. chinense*
SHU: 150,000–300,000

Pasado

4

The Pueblo Indians of New Mexico traditionally roasted, peeled, and dried the fruits of this chili—both green and red—to preserve it for use in winter. This concentrated the flavors, making them sweeter and hotter with a lingering smokiness, excellent when used in soups and stews. *Chile pasado* means "chili from the past."

Species: *C. annuum*
SHU: 1,000–10,000

Pasilla

3

The pasilla (meaning raisin) or *chile negro* (black chili) is normally found dried or powdered. In its fresh form it is known as *chilaca*, but in California it is often confused with the ancho and may be sold as pasilla even in its fresh form. The fruits grow to 7.8" (20cm) long and 2.3" (6cm) in diameter with a very dark green skin that dries to brown, almost black. Their sweet, dark, and smoky aroma lends a wonderfully rich flavor to sauces. Together with dried poblanos (ancho and *mulato*), it forms the trinity of chilies used in the Mexican national dish *mole*.

Species: *C. annuum*
SHU: 1,000–1,500

Peppadew

Johan Steenkamp discovered the Peppadew growing in the backyard of his holiday home in the Eastern Cape province of South Africa. The origins of this chili are unknown, but growing and processing it has grown to a global business, with the pepper being exported around the world. The fruits are about the size of cherry tomatoes and have a sweet flavor with a mild to hot bite. The success of the Peppadew shows what can be done with a chili that is well marketed. Seeds are not available commercially to the home grower.
Species: *C. annuum*
SHU: 1,100–1,200

Pepperoncini

Originally from Italy, the pepperoncini produces contorted fruits some 2.7–3.9" (7–10cm) in length that are sweet and mild, ideal for salads and pickling. They mature through orange to red, but are mostly used when they are still green.
Species: *C. annuum*
SHU: 100–500

Peter Pepper

This pepper has a most distinctive shape—once seen, it is never forgotten. It is grown principally as an ornamental plant (that makes an interesting conversation piece), but its thin-walled fruit, 3.9–5.8" (10–15cm) long and 0.7–1" (2–3cm) in diameter, has a good flavor and is excellent in salsas and stir-fries. Though some companies have made commercial sauces from this pepper, they are not widely available.
Species: *C. annuum*
SHU: 10,000–25,000

Pimiento

Not to be confused with the fruit commonly known as the "red pepper," there are many varieties of pimiento, including Perfection, Truhart Perfection, and Super Red. The heart-shaped fruits grow 3.1–5.8" (8–15cm) long and 1.5–3.1" (4–8cm) in diameter. Commercially grown for canning or bottling, they are used for their color and sweet flavor. Pimientos can be found bottled in supermarkets and are frequently sold as roasted peppers.
Species: *C. annuum*
SHU: 100–500

Pimiento de Padron

A delicacy from Galicia in Spain, *pimientos de padron* are sweet peppers, though about one in every eight can be hot. They are available from specialty shops and markets, but they taste best fresh from the garden. To prepare them, heat up a skillet, add a good dash of olive oil, turn up the heat, and add the fruit. Fry until they start to blister, then turn them into a bowl lined with a sheet of absorbent paper towel and add some coarsely ground sea salt. Eat them while they are hot, using the stem as a handle.
Species: *C. annuum*
SHU: 500–3,500

Piquin

The piquin, which grows wild in the highlands of Mexico, produces hundreds of very tiny, very hot oval fruits—between 0.4–0.7" (1–2cm) long and a mere 0.2" (5mm) in diameter. Despite the minute size, piquins pack a real punch at up to 40,000 SHU. They are good in stews, but you may want to fish them out of your plate before you eat.
Species: *C. annuum*
SHU: 30,000–40,000

Piros F1

A reliable, easy-to-grow hybrid of the Anaheim type, these plants grow to over 3ft (1m) in height and produce fruits 7–7.8" (18–20cm) long that ripen from green to red.
Species: *C. annuum*
SHU: 70,000–80,000

Poblano

The poblano has a large dark green, red, or purple fruit up to 4.6" (12cm) long and 3.1" (8cm) in diameter. A dried poblano is known as an ancho or *mulato*. Together with the pasilla, this makes up the trinity of chilies used in the Mexican national dish *mole*. Due to their size, poblanos are also ideal for making *chiles rellenos*.
Species: *C. annuum*
SHU: 1,000–2,000

Poinsettia

The fruits of this variety are arranged in a circle like flower petals and resemble a poinsettia bract once the green fruits have matured to deep red—hence the name. An ornamental plant, this variety produces thin, upright fruits, 2.3–3.5" (6–9cm) long and 0.4–0.7" (1–2cm) in diameter, that create an arresting contrast to the dark green foliage.
Species: *C. annuum*
SHU: 1,250–2,500

Prairie Fire

This tiny ornamental chili plant grows to only 5.9" (15cm) high, but can spread to 11.7–14.8" (30–38cm). It produces hundreds of small, conical fruits—0.6" (1.5cm) long and 0.2" (5mm) in diameter—that turn from yellow to orange and eventually a mature red. This is an excellent pot plant, ideal for a sunny location. Keep it in the kitchen for a ready supply—the hot fruit is great in stir-fries and in dishes that need a little boost.
Species: *C. annuum*
SHU: 1,000–1,500

Riot

This short, compact plant produces a riot of thin chilies 2–3.1" (5–8cm) long that protrude upward. The fruits turn from yellow to orange and bright red when ripe. Developed by Dr. Jim Baggett of Oregon State University, this is generally an ornamental pepper, but the fruit is edible, so don't let it go to waste.
Species: *C. annuum*
SHU: 50,000–75,000

Santa Fe Grande

The fruits of the Santa Fe Grande are most often sold and used in their unripe yellow form. If left to mature, they will ripen to red. This is a large, waxy, thick-walled, conical chili that grows 2.7–3.5" (7–9cm) long and 1–1.5" (3–4cm) in diameter, the fruits gently tapering to a point. The plants grow to 23.5" (60cm) in height. Commercially grown fruit are often canned or pickled, but they can also be eaten raw or cooked.

Species: *C. annuum*
SHU: 500–750

Scotch Bonnet

A relative of the habanero, the ferociously hot Scotch bonnet gets its innocent name from the shape of its fruit that resembles a tam-o'-shanter (a rimless woolen cap with a pom-pom that was worn in Scotland). Popular in the Caribbean, they form the main ingredient in Jamaican barbecue seasoning and are also excellent in pickles and chutneys. The irregularly shaped fruit is somewhat smaller and squatter than the habanero, grows to between 0.7–1.5" (2–4cm) long and 0.4–1" (1–3cm) in diameter, and can be found in various color combinations. Like the habanero, the Scotch bonnet can be hard to germinate and requires much sun if the fruit is to mature successfully. Common varieties include Scotch bonnet red, Big Sun (larger than usual fruits, up to 2.3" [6cm] long), and Burkina yellow.

Species: *C. chinense*
SHU: 100,000–300,000

Sebes

Originally from Czechoslovakia but also cultivated in parts of Hungary, Sebes produces large, flattened, banana-style fruits 3.9–5.9" (10–15cm) long and 0.4–1.5" (2–4cm) in diameter that mature from green to bright orange and are ideal for stuffing or frying.

Species: *C. annuum*
SHU: 1,000–2,500

Serrano

The serrano produces bullet-shaped fruits about 2–2.7" (5–7cm) long with a smooth skin. They are similar to the jalapeño in shape, but much smaller and more elongated. Due to their thin skin, they can be used directly without any preparation, and are ideal for most dishes. Hotter than the jalapeño and with a sharper taste, the fruits ripen from yellow through green to red. There are a number of varieties, including the slightly larger purple serrano, which turns a deep purple instead of red.
Species: *C. annuum*
SHU: 8,000–20,000

Shishito

The Japanese shishito is a small, wrinkled sweet pepper. It grows 3.1–3.9" (8–10cm) long and 0.7–1" (2–3cm) in diameter and is used as a garnish for Japanese dishes. The peppers are picked when still green and will turn bright red when they are left to ripen.
Species: *C. annuum*
SHU: 150–250

Super Chili F1

This small, compact plant produces an abundance of very hot 2–2.7" (5–7cm) elongated fruits that ripen from green through orange to red. It was the All-American Selections winner in 1998, which is tantamount to winning a chili Oscar for your variety.
Species: *C. annuum*
SHU: 20,000–40,000

Surinam Red

Both the red and yellow varieties probably originated in Surinam, South America, and both are extremely hot. In the Caribbean, the Surinam yellow is also known as the Madame Jeanette pepper. It produces the larger fruit and is closely related to the Scotch bonnet and habanero. Neither variety is recommended for growing in cool climates; they are hothouse plants outside the tropics.
Species: *C. chinense*
SHU: 250,000–500,000

Szentesi Semi-Hot

The Szentesi semi-hot from Hungary produces fruits that are 3.9–5.8" (10–15cm) long and 1–2.3" (3–6cm) in diameter, maturing from yellow through orange to red. They are very good for stuffing and roasting but are not easy to dry because of their thick flesh and firm skins.

Species: *C. annuum*
SHU: 1,250–2,500

Tabasco

The Tabasco chili is the key ingredient in Tabasco™ Sauce. The plant, which grows to 3ft (1m) in height, is a prolific producer with up to 100 fruits that grow pointing upward, which makes for an impressive sight. The fruits grow to between 1–1.5" (3–4cm) in length and about 0.4" (1cm) in diameter, starting a light yellow-green and changing to red when ripe. Such is the global success of the hot sauce brand that the chilies used by the McIlhenny Company are grown not only in Louisiana but as far afield as Venezuela and Guatemala.

Species: *C. frutescens*
SHU: 30,000–50,000

Takanotsume

From Japan comes the takanotsume, a compact plant that grows upright and produces very hot clusters of fruits, 2–2.7" (5–7cm) long and 0.4–0.6" (1–1.5cm) in diameter, that are mostly found dried as flakes or powder.

Species: *C. annuum*
SHU: 5,000–30,000

Tears of Fire

Expect a truly spectacular display from this prolific, ornamental conservatory plant. The fruit is initially green and then turns a rich brown before ripening to red. It can be cooked or used raw, but be careful: these chilies are hot.

Species: *C. annuum*
SHU: 25,000–35,000

Tepin 8

The tepin, also known as the chiltepin, or bird pepper, grows wild in Mexico, the southwestern USA, and some parts of Africa. The tiny fruit, just larger than a pea, is extremely hot. Germination is reported to take longer than that of domesticated chilies, but the plants will grow for many years if they are kept protected from frost.

Species: *C. annuum*
SHU: 40,000–50,000

Thai Dragon F1 9

This variety looks very similar to the Super Chili F1, except that the fruits grow *pendant* (hanging down). Thin-walled, they are 2.3–3.5" (6–9cm) long and 0.4–0.7" (1–1.5cm) in diameter, tapering to a point. The plant is easy to grow and produces hundreds of fruit that are easily dried for future use. Common in Thai cuisine, Thai dragons are good in stir-fries and can be added to the vinegar mixture when pickling onions to give them a little extra bite.

Species: *C. annuum*
SHU: 75,000–100,000

Tokyo Hot F1 7

A very prolific hybrid cayenne, these pencil-thin fruits ripen from dark green to red and grow up to 4.6" (12cm) long but are only 0.4–0.7" (1–1.5cm) in diameter.

Species: *C. annuum*
SHU: 20,000–30,000

Right: Chilies for sale in Port Louis, Mauritius.

CHILIES
IN THE KITCHEN

For most people, chili powder is their first experience with chilies in the kitchen. However, all is not what it seems. When buying commercial chili powders, it is best to check the list of ingredients and how the name of the product is spelled.

Commercial chili powder (which is still spelled "chili" powder in the UK, even though "chilli" is the standard spelling there) does not normally contain just chilies but is an imaginative combination of spices that may include chili, oregano, cumin, garlic, and more.

This blended chili powder was developed in 1890 by William Gebhardt, a German immigrant living in New Braunfels, Texas, who created the spice mixture to make the preparation of the popular spicy meat dish known as *chili* (*chile*) *con carne* (chili with meat) more convenient for the home cook.

Generic chili powder (actual chili powder, not the blend) can be made from a combination of different chilies, ground and mixed to provide a consistent level of heat. Generally, it is best to purchase a powder made from a chili variety you know. That way you can tell what to expect in the way of flavor and heat. You should be able to find cayenne pepper or jalapeño powder in most good supermarkets or grocery stores.

Right: Chilies can be added to almost any meal to spice up a bland dish or create an exciting taste sensation. Unless you are sure of the variety you are using, err on the side of caution and experiment carefully.

Storing fresh chilies

The best place for storing chilies is in the refrigerator (but not in a plastic bag, or they may rot), or in a cool, dark cupboard. If you store them with fruit, they will continue to ripen, and then rot.

Drying chilies

Dehydration is one of the simplest and oldest methods of preserving food items. The aim is to reduce the water content of the fruit and thus discourage the growth of bacteria and microbes. Chilies contain approximately 92 percent water, so dried ones will weigh a lot less than fresh ones do.

Dried chilies will keep for a year, after which they begin to lose their flavor. Keep the pods stored in an airtight container. I use zip-top bags from which I remove as much air as possible. Good-quality dried chilies should still be flexible, not brittle.

Air drying

Air drying is best done in a well-ventilated, protected area (such as a screened veranda or an airing cupboard, for example), where the fruit is shielded from pests. The process can take days or even weeks, depending on the conditions. Chilies have an elastic, watertight skin and will take a long time to dry whole. Use a skewer to make a few small holes in the skin to speed up the process.

Chilies are commonly dried after they have been strung together. If you choose to do it this way, be sure that the string pierces the stem of the chili and not the flesh. Strings like these are called *ristras* in Spanish and are sometimes displayed in delicatessen shops.

Left: Chilies can take some time to dry, depending on the weather conditions.

Sun drying

To sun dry your produce, you need warm temperatures, low humidity, and a constant breeze. After the drying is complete, you will need to apply a method of decontamination to kill any insects and their eggs. Commonly, sun-dried products are frozen or baked to do this. Unless you have the correct conditions, this method is not recommended for the home.

Oven drying

To dry chilies in your oven, place them on a wire rack. Set your oven to its lowest setting (on some gas cookers, just leaving the pilot light on will be enough). The temperature needs to be kept as low as possible, between 100–120°F (40–50°C), so you may need to keep the oven door ajar. The point is not to cook the chilies, as this will make them turn to mush when rehydrated. Fan ovens are excellent as they circulate the hot air, which speeds up the process. To make drying even quicker, you can slice your chilies into rings and dry them on a baking tray lined with a piece of greaseproof paper.

Dehydrators

You can dry chilies at home without any specialty equipment; all you need is an oven. If you are planning to dry large quantities regularly, then consider investing in a domestic dehydrator.

Rehydrating dried chilies

To rehydrate whole dried chilies, first clean off any dust with a tissue or wash them gently in fresh water. Then place them in a small bowl and cover with warm water. How long they take to rehydrate will depend on the type of chili you are using. Usually, the longer they are left to soak, the better. In most cases, an hour is adequate. The water can be discarded.

Right: If you buy dried chilies like this, it is best to clean them before use.

Smoking chilies

Traditional Mexican smoked chilies (chipotles) are made from red jalapeños. Any chili can be smoked, but the larger, fleshy ones are best, as they absorb more of the smoky flavor.

Smoking is an art form. A number of different smokers are available commercially; each works in a different way and requires more attention than you would expect. The simplest to operate is the Bradley smoker, which can be used for both hot and cold smoking and requires very little attention during the smoking process. Another type is the offset smoker, which has a separate firebox. If you don't have a fancy smoker, you can still smoke chilies in a kettle-style barbecue.

The aim is to dry and smoke the chilies over a long period of time. Remember that you do not wish to cook the flesh, as it will turn into a pulp as soon as the chilies are rehydrated.

It is not advisable to use any of the variety of small stove-top smokers designed to hot-smoke meat and fish. These tend to get too hot and will cook the chilies before they are dried. However, they can still be used to smoke pre-dried chilies using the following quick cheat:

The cheat's guide to smoked chilies

1. The cheat's method is to buy already dried chilies (or dry your own) and then smoke them. They will not attain the same depth of flavor, as the smoke will not have penetrated the flesh, but they are an excellent substitute if you want to make your own chili powder.

2. A second cheat, if you have a kettle-style barbecue, is to make a smoke pillow. Take hardwood chips (hickory, oak, or almost any fruit wood) and soak them in water for a few hours. Now take a piece of aluminum foil, approximately 24" (60cm) long and as wide, and fold it in half lengthways to make it double thick. Fold it in half again lengthways and then fold over the short sides to make a little bag. Place the soaked wood chips in the bag and seal the long edge with a secure fold. Now use a skewer or small knife to make a number of small holes in one side of the pillow. Build a small fire on one side of your kettle barbecue and place the smoke pillow, holes facing up, against the coals. The pillow will generate smoke and protect the rest of the barbecue from the direct heat of the fire. If you make several smoke pillows, you can replace them when they lose "steam." I find that smoking chilies for two or three hours imparts a very good flavor. Experiment, depending on how strong you want the flavor to be.

Cold smoking

To cold-smoke chilies for a full flavor requires time and patience. The fruit needs to be in the best possible condition—smoking is not what you do with leftover or damaged pods. A consistent source of warm smoke is required to dry and flavor the chilies. In a commercial smokehouse, the smoke generator is often separate from the smokehouse, a luxury we don't have for small-scale home smoking, so tend to your smoker regularly to ensure that you do not cook your chilies.

With the exception of the Bradley smoker, which can simply be turned on when it is needed, you need to prepare your smoker carefully and have extra fuel ready—this is going to be a long, slow process that can take up to two days. The final result should be pods that are hard but still pliable, with a reddish brown color.

You will need:

- 11–22 lb (5–10kg) charcoal or coal briquettes
- hardwood kindling
- hardwood chips or powder (hickory is best, but oak or almost any fruit tree wood will do)
- a kettle or offset barbecue
- lots of fresh red chilies

Above: These chilies have been smoked to perfection using cherry wood.

DO NOT use softwoods or any wood that has been treated with varnish, polish, or preservatives. Similarly, do not use pine wood, and never opt for the wood of any poisonous plant, such as oleander. Charcoal or coal briquettes are the best heat source, as they burn more consistently and controllably than wood. If you do wish to use wood, soak the wood chips or powder in water for a few hours before use; this ensures that they will smoke rather than burn.

In an offset smoker, build a small fire with charcoal or briquettes. If you are using a kettle-style barbecue, build a small fire on one side, then go and prepare the chilies.

1. Wash the pods to remove any unwanted pests and dirt.
2. Using a small skewer, pierce the chilies near the shoulder and again at the tip. This will speed up the drying process.
3. Place the chilies as far as possible from the source of the heat and close the lid of your barbecue.
4. Adjust the vents on your barbecue so that the fire continues to smolder but does not go out (this is much harder than it sounds).
5. Check the barbecue every hour, adding more wood chips and charcoal as necessary.
6. Every few hours, you will need to turn the chilies over and move them around on the grill.
7. Carefully inspect the chilies from time to time: you do NOT want to cook them.

Right: If you prefer, you can grind your chili powder much finer than this.

Making chili powder

Making chili powder can be a dangerous sport if it is not done correctly, as I found out when I was developing our range of hot rubs and crisp flavors! Since then I have been seen wearing swimming goggles and an air filter—or what I call a painter's mask—when making larger batches for sampling. It pays to remember that chili powder can escape from almost any device you try to grind it in.

The best method is to use an ordinary blender (with a glass jug), with a sealing layer of cling-film wrap placed over the top before the lid is pushed on tightly. After grinding, remember that when you pour the powder into a storage jar, it will again become airborne, hence the need for goggles.

You can grind chilies as fine as you like. For very fine powders, avoid grinding up the seeds, as they make for a slight bitterness, but they are excellent in a coarsely ground mixture and make it look very attractive.

It is best to grind chilies that are very dry, because otherwise they will clump. If you are unsure, place them in your oven/dehydrator until they are hard.

Pickling chilies

A traditional method of preserving food is pickling by using a pickling medium, such as vinegar, which contains a mild acid that prevents the growth of bacteria. Before pickling, chilies are often immersed in a brine (salt solution) to draw out some of the water that would otherwise dilute the vinegar and thus slow the pickling process. Adding salt to the pickling solution also helps to reduce the water content of the chilies.

Pickling solution

- 2 cups (500ml) water
- 2 cups (500ml) distilled vinegar
- 2 tsp non-iodized salt

Place the ingredients in a large pan and bring to a boil. Use a skewer to make a few holes at each end of the chilies if you intend on pickling whole fruit, to allow the pickling solution to enter each chili. Layer the chilies in a sealable jar and cover with the hot pickling solution, ensuring that they are completely covered.

The pickling process will take around two to three weeks. Pickled chilies should keep for at least a year if the jars are stored in a cool, dark place.

Please note that some recipes may require you to roast and skin the chilies before pickling them. This is because some varieties—such as the ancho, for example—have a tough outer skin that is best removed.

Above: Pickled chilies.

Bottling chili sauces

Making your own sauces and bottling them is easy. It is also a lot of fun to experiment with different ingredients. Store bottling jars in a clean, dry place until you are ready to use them. To ensure that your sauces keep, sterilize all jars or bottles each time before use by boiling them in hot water. Be sure to sterilize the caps as well and line each one with a seal (cut slightly larger than the lid) made of greaseproof paper.

Whatever the recipe you are preparing, all sauces should be cooked for a minimum of five minutes after reaching the boiling point to kill any bacteria before they have a chance to ruin your sauce.

1. While your sauce is bubbling away on the stove, you must begin to sterilize the bottling jars you wish to use. Choose a pot that is deep enough to cover the selected sauce bottles with water completely.
2. Place a small wire rack in the bottom to keep the jars from resting directly on the base of the pot.
3. Stand the jars on the wire rack in the pot and fill with water, ensuring that the water fills all the bottles and covers them completely.
4. Turn up the heat and boil for at least 5 minutes.
5. Once the sauce is ready, remove one of the bottles from the water using tongs and fill it. Use a funnel to do this so that you don't scald yourself, but remember that it, too, will have to have been sterilized in boiling water.

Ladle the sauce from the cooking pot while it is still boiling, directly into the funnel. It is advisable to use a clean towel to hold each bottle while filling it—again so that there is no chance that you might burn yourself.

When the bottle is filled, screw on the lined cap and invert the bottle to seal it.

Most sauces made this way contain vinegar, lemon juice, or lime juice as a base ingredient to raise the acidity level and prevent microbial growth. Bottled sauces should last up to nine months—the flavor will develop as they age.

Be suspicious when a bottle you have just opened makes a fizzing sound, bubbles, or has an unpleasant smell. This is usually an indication that it was not sufficiently sterilized. In such cases it is best to discard the sauce immediately—do not even think of trying it.

Right: Chutneys, jams, and pickles—chilies are versatile.

Chilies in alcohol

For an unusual taste, you could pickle chilies in alcohol. Preserving chilies in alcohol has two effects: it produces an interesting drink and also preserves the chilies for later use. I have a few bottles of chili vodka that were sent to me from Canada. Each contains two 911 chilies. I kept them until the fruits started to turn a nice red color; after three years I could wait no longer and tried it. WOW! I coughed and spluttered, and it was a few minutes before I was able to speak again. The concoction is far too strong to consume at room temperature, so now it lies in wait in the freezer until I find someone brave enough to try it!

I have also recently tried chili sherry—and not for cooking, as I normally would—which makes a very pleasant drink. The secret, it seems, is to dilute the chili sherry with six times its volume of normal sherry. The result is a fantastic, warming drink.

Freezing chilies

Frozen chilies do not reconstitute well when defrosted, because freezing ruptures the cells of the fruit and causes them to turn mushy. However, freezing is an excellent idea if you are going to cook with your chilies, for they lose none of their flavor or heat.

Blend excess chilies in a blender using a little water, and pour the result into ice trays or even ice bags. When a little heat is needed, just let one dissolve in the pan—as simple as frozen peas! Sauce and pickle manufacturers have freezers full of chilies in bags, frozen on trays before bagging, ready to be made into sauces and pickles. In this way, the chilies are easier to separate when just a few are needed.

The kitchen garden

Growing chilies is fairly simple and very rewarding: just a few plants can provide enough pods to keep most people going through the season. You can grow them in window boxes or in pots, have them standing in your kitchen, or place them in any other sunny spot. Although you can retain seeds from your plants, the ease with which chilies cross-pollinate means that you are unlikely to be growing what you expected. If you visit a seed producer, you will see plants growing in their own tents in greenhouses. This is done as much to ensure that they produce pure single-variety seeds and cannot cross-pollinate with any neighboring plants as it is to protect them from the elements.

If you are thinking of growing chilies from seed, I recommend that you get them from a reputable company that has some expertise in chilies. Seeds will keep for up to five years in a cool, dry environment.

Growing from seed

If you have a garden with a sunny spot, get an early start and germinate your seeds as soon as possible. Spring is usually best, but inquire at your local nursery or garden center if you are unsure of the best time to plant for your specific climate.

Chili seeds require constant heat to germinate, so to ensure the best chances of germination, they must be kept at between 77–86°F (25–30°C). Place the seeds in small pots or seedling trays, two to three seeds per pot, with a little good potting soil (potting compost). Light is not important until the seedlings finally appear, but the soil must be kept moist, so don't put the trays in an airing cupboard and then forget about them.

1. Most seeds will germinate within 10 days, but be patient—some can take weeks. Pick out the strongest seedlings and place these in larger (3–4"/8–10cm) pots. They will need to be kept in a warm, light area: on a windowsill or in a warm conservatory is best.

2. Once the plants reach 4–6" (10–15cm) in height, you can repot them into larger containers.
3. Mix a little well-aged manure or compost into the soil to ensure that your chilies don't lack any essential nutrients. Alternatively, inquire at your local garden center or nursery about a good plant food and use as recommended by the manufacturer.
4. If you live in an area that experiences mild winters, then it is safe to leave your chili plants outside—well-covered nonetheless. In cold areas, move your chilies indoors and water sparingly but regularly. They may lose most of their leaves, but they should sprout again. Prune back old growth in spring and fertilize.

It is possible to grow chilies outdoors in the northern hemisphere, but remember that they need the same environment as tomatoes; a greenhouse or polytunnel will usually provide great results. In my conservatory, I have a basic hydroponics system from Greenhouse Sensation. The plants are placed into the system when they have grown to 4–6" (10–15cm), and the results have been excellent. The bottom line is: protection from the cold is essential.

Unless you just want fabulous and extravagant foliage, it is best to let the plants start fruiting before you provide them with a full dose of fertilizer. In the hydroponics system, plants enjoy a constant trickle of water and a proprietary nutrient mix. I initially start with a full dose, weaken it until the fruit is set, and then return to a full-strength mixture.

For pot- or bag-grown chilies, you can use feed that is recommended for tomatoes, watering each day and following the manufacturer's instructions; normally the plants need to be fed once a week.

Right: Polytunnel farming on a commercial scale.

Variety selection

Selecting which varieties to grow depends on where you live, what facilities you have available, and, of course, your taste. Some plants can grow to a tremendous size and will require constant attention (as well as watering, etc.). If you are looking for small, compact varieties with a good crop of hot chilies, then Super Chili F1 and Thai dragon are good starting points. Poblano and Anaheim chilies, on the other hand, will occupy more space and are not suitable for small home gardens.

Unless you live in a warm climate, habanero and the other super-hot varieties can be a bit disappointing. They can be hard to germinate and take a long time to fruit.

It may pay off to find a local expert who can give you advice about what varieties are best for the area in which you live. There are many chili fans out there, and therefore many chili-related websites that can provide seeds and give advice on growing them. Some of the best suggestions come from keen amateurs.

Right: Chilies make attractive container plants for the smaller garden and in the kitchen.

CHILI RECIPES

In the course of my travels, my taste buds have been subjected to almost every culinary assault imaginable. Once, in Berkeley, California, I was invited to a Thai restaurant where each course was hotter than the one before. I survived, but only just, thanks to the valuable training received at my local Indian restaurant.

I was the target of countless ethnic dishes, and it seemed at times as though my hosts were vying with each other to see who could do the most damage to my palate. Chili peppers were the common denominator in all of the most memorable events.

At home I began to experiment with gusto. I once bought a tray of fresh chilies, washed them, cut them into rings, and pickled them in vinegar—without protecting my hands. That night I could hardly move my fingers. Although I washed my hands again and again and lathered on copious amounts of cream, the discomfort lasted for nearly 12 hours. It was a lesson well learned.

Over the next 15 years or so, I collected and tried many chili recipes. I present to you here my favorite ones, together with some fine additions from fellow chili fanatics Derryck Strachan, Chilli Pepper Pete, and Andy Teo. In many cases, no particular variety is specified, because I feel that it is a matter of choice. If you like your food hot, then choose one of the more ferocious chilies; if you like it milder, then select a gentler burn.

Right: Chilies are an acquired taste, so unless you are used to them, or are feeling particularly brave, start with milder varieties and gradually work your way up to the seriously hot ones.

SPICE
MIXES,
SAUCES,
AND
SALSAS

Basic curry powder

I have eaten many curries, and some have been really bad. The secret of a good curry is in the powder you use! Over the years I have tried most spice combinations, and the recipe below is for a basic but rich curry powder. Feel free to adapt it; I have listed a number of options you may wish to add.

Ingredients:

Whole spices:

- 10 red dried chilies
- 10 tsp coriander seeds
- 6 tsp cumin seeds
- 3 tsp fenugreek seeds
- 2 tsp black mustard seeds
- 2 tsp black peppercorns
- 4 cardamom pods

Ground spices:

- 1 tsp ground turmeric
- 1 tsp ground ginger

Optional:

- 4–6 curry leaves
- 1–2 tsp white mustard seeds
- 1 tsp cinnamon
- 6–8 whole clove
- 1–2 tsp caraway seeds
- ¼ tsp fennel seeds
- ½ tsp nutmeg
- ½ tsp horseradish powder

Instructions:

Remove stems and seeds from the chilies and then dry roast, together with all of the whole spices, in a thick-bottomed pan over medium heat. A high-sided pan is best as some of the spices will pop when they heat up. Dry roast for 5–10 minutes, keeping the spices moving so they don't burn. The aroma is great and the flavors will be much more intense.

Place the hot spices in a blender or spice grinder and grind to a powder. You can also use a mortar and pestle. Now add the turmeric and ginger powder. Allow to cool before storing.

This mixture is best used within a few days, but can be stored in an airtight container in a cool, dark place for several weeks.

Berberé

Berberé comes from Ethiopia. It is a dry spice mix and has become the basis for most Ethiopian cuisine. It is often made into a paste or sauce with the addition of oil, wine, or water. *Berberé* makes a fantastic bread dip. It can also be used as a chicken marinade, either wet or dry, prior to roasting.

Ingredients:

- 1 tsp allspice berries
- 3 tsp cardamom pods
- 16–20 cloves
- 4–5 tsp fenugreek seeds
- 2 tsp black pepper
- 1 tsp turmeric powder
- 4–5 tsp cayenne pepper powder
- 1 tsp salt

Instructions:

Dry fry all of the spices for a few minutes to bring out their special flavors, remembering to keep them moving all the time. Allow to cool and then grind with mortar and pestle, or in a blender, adding the salt, turmeric, and cayenne a little at a time. This dry form of berberé can be stored in the fridge in an airtight container until needed.

To make this into a paste, add fresh ingredients, such as finely chopped onions or ginger, to oil, water, or wine and blend to a fine paste. Store in an airtight container in the fridge, with a little oil poured over the top to keep air out and preserve it for longer.

Harissa

Harissa comes from North Africa and the Middle East. It is a smooth paste made from dried chilies, garlic, and olive oil, but can include other spices such as caraway, cumin, coriander seeds, and salt. Available ready-made in most good delicatessen shops, it is very simple to make and adapt to your tastes.

Ingredients:

- 2–3 large dried red chilies
- 2 garlic cloves
- 1 tsp caraway seeds
- 1 tsp cumin, ground
- 1 tsp coriander seeds, ground
- ¼ tsp salt
- olive oil

Instructions:

Soak the dried chilies in warm water for an hour or until reconstituted. Remove excess water and dry with paper towels. Place in a blender with the garlic, caraway, cumin, coriander seeds, and a little salt and blend to a smooth paste. You can add a little olive oil at this stage if required.

Place in a small jar and cover with a very thin layer of the olive oil. It will keep in the fridge for a few weeks.

Chipotles in adobo

Chipotles are a staple in many Mexican dishes, and every week I am asked to supply them. I have only ever seen them in cans (tins), so I am very pleased to have Derryck Strachan's recipe in my book.

Ingredients:

- 6 chipotles
- 1 large onion, chopped
- 6 garlic cloves
- 6 tbsp cider vinegar
- 6 tbsp tomato ketchup
- 2 tbsp dark brown sugar
- salt
- 2 cups (450ml) water
- 1 tbsp vegetable oil
- allspice, cinnamon, cumin (to taste)
- 3–4 tbsp lime juice

Instructions:

Place the chipotles in a pan with half the onion, 5 garlic cloves, cider vinegar, tomato ketchup, brown sugar, water, vegetable oil, and the spices. Bring to a boil and then simmer over a low heat for about 20 minutes or until the chilies are soft and the mixture has begun to thicken.

Remove the chili mixture from the heat and add the rest of the onion and garlic. Stir in the lime juice and season with spices and salt.

Keeps in the fridge for about a week.

Zhoug

This is a delicious Middle Eastern pesto, typical of Yemeni cuisine. Add it to soups or use as a salad dressing or condiment.

Ingredients:

- 3 oz (75g) parsley
- 2 oz (50g) cilantro (coriander) leaves, fresh
- 2 garlic cloves
- 1 tsp cumin, ground
- 1 tsp cayenne
- 1 tsp salt
- 1 tsp pepper
- 1 oz (25g) fresh chilies (the hotter the better)

Instructions:

Put all the ingredients into a blender and mix well. Will keep for a week if stored in the fridge.

Mother's warm tomato chutney

This chutney recipe has been in my family for years. It is very simple to make and always turns out great.

Ingredients:

- 4.4 lb (2kg) tomatoes
- 4 medium size onions, finely chopped
- 1 lb (500g) brown sugar
- 2 tbsp dry English mustard powder
- 1 ½ tbsp curry powder
- 1 ½ tbsp flour
- 1–2 tsp cayenne pepper
- brown malt vinegar
- salt as needed

Instructions:

Skin the tomatoes, cut into pieces the size of walnuts, and sprinkle with salt (to draw out the excess liquid). Add the chopped onions and soak the mixture overnight.

In the morning, pour off the liquid and discard, spoon the tomato and onion mixture into a pot, and just cover with vinegar. Boil for 15 minutes.

Mix the dry ingredients (sugar, mustard powder, curry powder, flour, cayenne pepper) in cold vinegar to make a thick paste. Add to the tomato and onion mixture, stir well to mix, and simmer over a low heat for about 45 minutes until thick, stirring occasionally.

Pour into sterilized jars and cover with lids while still hot. To allow the full flavors to develop, wait at least 2–3 months before you open a jar to enjoy your homemade chutney.

Lemon 'n' lime fire chutney

This is a very sharp, citrus-flavored chutney, ideal on baked (jacket) potatoes or as a dip with curry. Instead of the limes and lemons, you could use grapefruit and oranges.

Ingredients:

- 6 limes
- 2 large lemons
- 1 lb (500g) onions, finely chopped
- 2 oz (50g) salt
- 1 lb (500g) sugar
- 3 cups (700ml) vinegar
- 2 tsp mustard seeds
- 2 tsp paprika
- 2 tsp ground cumin
- 1 tsp ground turmeric
- 20 hot bird's-eye (Thai) chilies, finely chopped in a blender or food processor
- 16 oz (200g) raisins

Instructions:

Place the limes and lemons in a pan and cover with water. Bring to a boil and simmer for 2–3 minutes, then leave to stand until cool enough to handle. Cut the fruit into halves and squeeze the juice into a bowl, removing the seeds. Chop the remaining skin and pulp into small pieces with scissors or a sharp knife, mix in the onions, and sprinkle with salt.

In a large pan, bring the vinegar and sugar to a boil and simmer until all the sugar has dissolved. Add the chopped lime, lemon, and onion mixture as well as all the dry spices, raisins, and chilies, mix well, and simmer for 2–3 hours, stirring frequently until the mixture has reduced by about 50 percent.

Pour into sterilized jars and seal while still hot. Your chutney will be ready to eat within 3–4 weeks.

The above recipe should make about 3 pints (1.5l) of chutney.

Jolly chili pickle

These tasty pickles can be served with savories as a snack and can also be served as a spicy side dish with any main meal.

Ingredients:

- 2.2 lb (1kg) large chilies
- 2 tbsp salt
- 1 tbsp turmeric, ground
- 2 tbsp black mustard seeds
- ½ cup (125ml) vinegar
- 2 tbsp garlic, chopped
- 2 cups (500ml) mustard oil
- 1 tsp fenugreek seeds
- 2 tsp nigella seeds
- 2 tsp asafetida, crushed

Instructions:

Wash and dry the chilies. Remove the stems and cut up the chilies. Sprinkle with salt and turmeric, toss to mix evenly, cover, and leave in the sun for two days. Soak mustard seeds in vinegar overnight, then grind in an electric blender with the garlic. Heat the oil and add the fenugreek and nigella seeds.

Stir and fry until the fenugreek is golden brown. Add the asafetida, stir, and then add the blended mixture and the chilies together with the liquid that will have gathered. Simmer, stirring now and then until oil rises and chilies are cooked. Cool and pour into sterilized jars.

Burning hot mango pickle

This oil pickle with mangoes is presented here the way they would make it in India. The mangoes are so unripe that the seeds are easy to cut through.

Ingredients:

- 12 green mangoes
- 50 fresh green chilies
- coarse salt
- 3 cups (750ml) malt vinegar
- 2 tsp fenugreek seeds
- 25 garlic cloves, peeled
- 4 oz (125g) fresh ginger root, sliced
- 2 oz (60g) cumin, ground
- 2 oz (60g) coriander seeds, ground

- 5 ¼ cups (1.25l) mustard oil or vegetable oil
- 2 tbsp black mustard seeds
- 2 tbsp fresh curry leaves
- 2 tbsp fennel seeds
- 1 tbsp nigella seeds
- 1 tbsp turmeric, ground
- 1 tbsp chili powder
- salt

Instructions:

Wash and dry the mangoes and cut them into six or eight sections, through the seed. Cut the chilies in half. Sprinkle mangoes and chilies with salt; spread out on a large, flat basket and leave to dry in the sun for three days.

Soak fenugreek seeds in some vinegar overnight, then combine with garlic, ginger, cumin, and coriander seeds in a blender. Blend to a smooth purée, adding just enough vinegar to facilitate blending.

Heat the oil in a non-aluminum pan and add mustard seeds, curry leaves, fennel seeds, and nigella seeds. When the mustard seeds stop popping, stir in the turmeric, chili powder, and blended mixture. Fry, stirring constantly for a few minutes. Add the salted mangoes, chilies, and remaining vinegar. Bring to a boil; reduce heat and simmer uncovered for about 30 minutes. Add salt to taste.

Cool the mixture and bottle in sterile jars. There should be enough oil to cover the top of the pickle. Cover with non-metallic lids and always use a dry spoon when taking a pickle from the jar.

Note: Use 1 lb (500g) dried mango instead of the fresh mangoes in this recipe and bypass the salting and drying process.

Hot Juan's BBQ rub

This sauce will not burn in the intense heat of charcoal or gas grills, and it's not only good for meat: it has been added to tomato soup, baked beans, steamed vegetables, garlic bread, and homemade bread—all with excellent results.

Ingredients:

- 1 tsp paprika (for color, not heat)
- 1 tsp garlic granules
- 1 tsp black pepper, finely ground
- ½ tsp dried basil

- ⅓ tsp cumin, ground
- ⅔ tsp chili powder (it is best to select a single-chili variety)
- ⅔ tsp salt

Instructions:

Place all the ingredients in a blender and blend to a fine powder. Lightly coat chicken, pork, or fish and allow to marinate for an hour before use.

If you add two parts of sugar to one part of BBQ rub, you can use the mixture to coat pork before roasting in the oven or in a barbecue using an indirect heat method. If you wish to use it on beef, omit the salt.

Cascabel and grapefruit sauce

This thin sauce makes a wonderful marinade for tuna or meat and will keep in the fridge for up to a month in a sealed container.

Ingredients:

- 24 cascabel chilies
- 4 ¼ cups (1l) water
- 4 ¼ cups (1l) grapefruit juice
- 1 cup (250ml) orange juice
- 3 tsp allspice
- 1 tsp salt
- 3–4 cloves of garlic, finely chopped

Instructions:

Dry roast the chilies for 3–4 minutes, keeping them moving so that they do not burn. Add the chilies to the water and simmer for 20 minutes, and then leave to cool.

Place water and chilies in a blender with half the grapefruit juice as well as the garlic and allspice. Strain the mixture and then add the rest of the juices.

Quick enchilada sauce

This delicious enchilada sauce can be made ahead of time—
it only takes about 15 minutes to prepare—and makes a
tasty hot sauce for many meat recipes.

Ingredients:

- 2 tbsp chili powder
- olive oil
- 1 large onion, very finely chopped
- 2 garlic cloves, crushed
- 3 tsp flour
- 9 oz (250g) tomato passata (uncooked tomato purée, also called sieved tomatoes)
- ½ cup (100ml) water

Instructions:

Lightly fry the onion and garlic in a little oil until
translucent. Remove from the pan and set aside.

Reduce the heat to low. Add another 2–3 tablespoons of oil,
then the flour, and mix well, using a whisk, until you have
a fine paste that contains absolutely no lumps. Now add the
chili powder and tomato passata and whisk again.

Simmer for a few minutes to thicken, adding water if
necessary. Return the onions and garlic to the sauce and
simmer for another minute. The sauce can be used straight
away or stored in the fridge for a few days.

Spoon over enchiladas, on pasta, or have with bangers and
mash—let your imagination lead you.

Fresh fruit salsa

It's a hot day—time to sit in the sun and enjoy a barbecue. But how about something a little different? This fruit salsa is great as a dip and can also be used on the barbecue. Spread some inside a whole fish before you grill it, and enjoy a taste sensation!

Ingredients:

- 1 large orange
- 1 large apple
- 1 kiwi (kiwifruit)
- 1–2 onions, chopped
- 1–2 chilies, sliced and seeded
- 1 garlic clove, crushed
- juice of one lime or lemon
- a few mint leaves
- salt and pepper

Instructions:

Peel and segment the orange, removing any unwanted seeds. Core and slice the apple. Peel and slice the kiwi. Put all of the fruit into a blender together with the chopped onion, crushed garlic, chilies, lime juice, and mint leaves.

Blend to a coarse but even consistency and then add salt and pepper to taste. Serve as a condiment for strong fish or as a salsa for dipping.

Habanero hot sauce

This recipe is simple to make, and the product can be bottled and stored.

Ingredients:

- 12 habaneros
- 1 yellow pepper— roasted, skinned, seeded, and chopped
- 1 onion, chopped
- 2–3 garlic cloves, chopped
- ½ cup (125ml) cider vinegar or white wine vinegar
- 6 tbsp lime juice
- a little water

Instructions:

Sauté onions and garlic, add the yellow pepper, and then add some water. Simmer on a low heat until the peppers have softened, then place in a blender with the habaneros and blend to a fine purée. Return to the pan, add the lime juice and vinegar, and simmer for a few minutes more. Store in clean, sterilized bottles in a dark, cool place.

Salsa cruda

This basic, uncooked salsa recipe makes a good base from which you can experiment with your own ingredients.

Ingredients:

- 2–3 garlic cloves, chopped
- 1 small to medium onion, chopped
- 1–2 fresh jalapeños, chopped
- 5–8 tomatoes, cubed
- 3 tbsp fresh cilantro (coriander) leaves, chopped
- cumin, ground and roasted
- lime juice to taste
- salt and pepper

Instructions:

Place all the ingredients in a blender, holding back 2–3 tomatoes, and blend to a fine consistency. Place the mixture in a bowl, chop up the remaining tomatoes, and add to the mix to give your salsa a more chunky texture.

Sambal oelek

From Southeast Asia comes this sambal that can be used to add fire and flavor to all sorts of dishes, such as soups and stir-fries. I have seen variations with garlic, tamarind water, and even lime juice—so be creative and experiment a little for a completely new taste.

Ingredients:

- 10–15 cayenne or bird's-eye (Thai) chilies
- dash of lemon juice
- 1–2 tsp salt

Instructions:

Using a mortar and pestle, pound the chilies to a fine paste, adding the salt a little at a time during the process. Add the lemon juice and mix. The paste will keep in the fridge for a few weeks, but can also be frozen for longer storage.

Teo chili condiment

This is a simple but very tasty condiment my friend Andy Teo recommends. It can add that special something to a meal of plain, steamed rice and chicken, or any other dish, for that matter.

Ingredients:

- 2–3 bird's-eye (Thai) or cayenne chilies
- a splash of sesame oil
- white wine vinegar or lemon juice to taste
- soy sauce to taste

Instructions:

Slice the chilies thinly, removing any loose seeds. Place in a small serving bowl and add the sesame oil, lemon juice or white wine vinegar, and some good-quality soy sauce until the mixture is to your liking.

Vizcaina

This traditional Basque chili sauce is usually served with salted cod fish, but it is also very good with chicken.

Ingredients:

- ½ lb (250g) onions
- 2 oz (50g) choricero (or ancho) chili, soaked
- 3 oz (75g) parsley, chopped fine
- 3 garlic cloves
- 1 tsp Spanish paprika
- 1 cup (250ml) chicken stock
- salt and pepper
- olive oil

Instructions:

Sauté the onions in the olive oil until soft, then add the garlic, paprika, and chili and simmer for a few minutes. Place in a blender with the stock and finely chopped parsley and blend until smooth. Add salt and pepper to taste. Store in the fridge in a sealed container.

Chili mustard

This semi-wholegrain mustard gets its heat from the chilies and mustard flour and its sweetness from the rice wine vinegar. It is ideally served with cold meats and sausages.

Ingredients:

- 2 oz (50g) white mustard seeds
- ½ cup (100ml) rice wine vinegar
- 2 tbs olive oil
- 2 tsp mustard powder
- 2 tsp chili powder

Instructions:

Soak the mustard seeds overnight in rice wine vinegar. Place this with all the other ingredients in a blender and blend until most of the seeds are broken.

Store in a small jar, best kept in the fridge.

Sambal bajak

Sambals are cold savory sauces, or dips, that are commonly served with Asian food. This particular one is a fried version that goes well with rice and can also be added to dishes that could use a little kick.

Ingredients:

- 10 chilies
- 2 small onions, coarsely chopped
- 3 garlic cloves
- 12 macadamia nuts (or candle nuts)
- 1 tsp galangal powder
- 1 tsp shrimp paste
- 3 tsp sugar
- ½ cup (125ml) tamarind water
- 1 oz (25g) coconut cream
- 2 tbs oil
- salt to taste

Instructions:

Blend chilies, onion, garlic, and nuts to a coarse paste. Add the galangal, shrimp paste, and sugar and blend again. Heat the oil in a small frying pan and fry the mixture for a few minutes. Add the tamarind water, coconut cream, and a little salt and simmer over low heat until the mixture starts to thicken. Place in a small jar and, once cool, store in the fridge.

HOT DISHES

Chilli Pepper Pete's red bean soup

This delicious soup makes the perfect warmer on a cold day. Serve it on its own or with fresh bread and watch the winter blues disappear.

Ingredients:

- 1 can red kidney beans, drained
- 1 large onion, finely chopped
- 2 tsp Mexican oregano
- 2 garlic cloves, crushed and chopped
- 1 lb (500g) fresh tomatoes
- 2 soaked chipotles
- 2 soaked anchos
- 1 tbsp olive oil
- salt and pepper
- grated cheese for the topping

Instructions:

Roast the tomatoes at 356°F (180°C) for 45 minutes and sauté the onions in olive oil until soft. Add the garlic and simmer for a further few minutes. Place tomatoes, garlic, onions, beans, oregano, and chipotles in a blender and mix until smooth. Pass through a sieve to remove any seeds and skin, place in a pan, and cook over a gentle heat.

Fry the anchos in a little olive oil and cut into strips. Add these to the soup and season with salt and pepper to taste. Spoon into bowls and top with a little grated cheese.

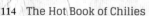

Watercress and poblano soup

The addition of a little roasted poblano gives this soup a subtle bite.

Ingredients:

- 1 large bunch watercress, washed
- 4 potatoes, peeled and finely sliced
- 1 large onion, finely chopped
- 3–4 sticks of celery, finely chopped
- 2 carrots, finely chopped
- 1 poblano or ancho, roasted (see below)
- olive oil to fry the onion
- 2 cups (500ml) chicken stock
- sour cream (optional)

Instructions:

Sauté the onions in a little olive oil in a large pan over low heat. When they turn translucent, add the potatoes, celery, and carrots and fry for a few minutes before adding the chicken stock. Increase the heat to a simmer. Chop the roasted chili and add. When the potatoes are done, add the watercress and simmer for a further 2–3 minutes. Remove from the heat and mix in a blender until the soup is smooth. Serve immediately with a dash of sour cream.

Chilaquile

This popular Mexican casserole provides a tasty way to use up old, stale corn tortillas by alternating layers of tortilla strips with layers of a rich, spicy tomato sauce topped with cheese. The stack is baked in the oven and served with crème fraiche or sour cream.

Ingredients:

- 6–8 corn tortillas
- 2 x 1 lb (450g) cans of quality chopped tomatoes
- 1 medium onion, chopped
- ½ cup (100ml) chicken stock
- 2–3 jalapeños or chipotles
- 7 oz (200g) grated cheddar cheese or similar
- oil for frying
- crème fraiche or sour cream

Instructions:

First fry the tortillas in a little oil for about 10–15 seconds on each side to stop them from falling apart. The frying pan needs to be large enough to fit a whole flat tortilla. Set aside and drain on a paper towel. Fry the onion over a low heat until it becomes translucent.

Add chopped tomatoes, chilies, and finally the chicken stock. Simmer for a further 5–6 minutes.

Tear the tortillas into strips and place a layer in a greased baking dish. Cover the tortillas with some tomato sauce and end with a layer of cheese. Continue in this way until you have used all the sauce and tortillas.

Place in a preheated oven at 356°F (180°C) for 15–20 minutes. When done, remove from the oven and serve immediately with a dollop of crème fraiche or sour cream.

If you like to experiment, then vary this recipe by adding other ingredients, such as beans, chicken, or mincemeat.

Doro wat

If you have made the *berberé* (see page 90), then you'll want a traditional Ethiopian dish to go with it. *Doro wat* is a stew spiced with *berberé* that contains chicken and hard-boiled eggs. There are many variations of this dish. This is a particularly easy one.

Ingredients:

- 1 lb (400g) chicken breast, chopped into small cubes
- 4 large onions, chopped
- 8 tsp berberé, dry or wet
- ½ cup (100ml) oil or 5 oz (150g) butter
- 4 hard-boiled eggs
- ¼ tsp black pepper
- ¼ tsp garlic powder or fresh garlic
- ½ tsp ginger, fresh or ground

- ¾ cup (200ml) red wine
- 2 cups (500ml) water
- salt
- juice of one lime or lemon

Variations:

- 2–3 tsp tomato purée
- 3–4 tsp peanut butter
- chicken stock to replace the water

Instructions:

Place the chicken in a bowl and pour over the lime or lemon juice. Use a little of the butter or oil in a large, ovenproof pan to brown the onions. Add the rest of the fat and all the spices. Simmer for a minute or two, stirring well. Add the wine and ½ cup (150ml) of the water and boil for a few minutes, again stirring well.

Add the chicken, making sure it gets well coated, and gently cook for 30–40 minutes. Add more water if required, a little salt to taste, and the hard-boiled eggs. Stir gently and return to the stove (hob) for a further 10 minutes at a low simmer or until the chicken is done.

This dish is best served with flatbread. In Ethiopia, *injera* is eaten with it. If you cannot find *injera*, then pita bread, tortillas, or even a chunk of fresh crusty bread makes a good alternative.

Creamy chicken curry

In this recipe, I use coconut milk to give it a creamy texture, and red onions because they are milder in flavor (for the curry powder, see page 88). This delicious curry is cooked slowly over a low heat—a large pan with a tight lid is best—and will take about 1–2 hours to prepare

Ingredients:

- 2.2–3 lb (1–1.5kg) chicken pieces (drumsticks or thighs)
- 4 medium red onions, halved and thinly sliced
- 1 small cauliflower, cut into small florets
- 9 oz (250g) mushrooms, cut into quarters
- ½ cup (150ml) coconut milk
- 4–5 celery sticks, chopped
- 4–5 tsp curry powder
- 2 oz (50g) ground almonds
- 2 oz (50g) raisins
- 4 cloves garlic, crushed
- olive oil for frying

Instructions:

Add a little oil to the pan and place over a low heat. When it is hot, add the onions, chicken, and curry powder, turn up the heat, and fry until the chicken has lightly browned.

Reduce the heat again to a low simmer and add all the other ingredients except the cauliflower. Simmer for about an hour and then add the cauliflower for the last 20 minutes.

Serve with rice or naan bread.

Mole poblano

This simple version of the popular and tasty Mexican dish does not call for any hard-to-find ingredients. You may also be able to buy ready-made *mole* sauce from a specialty retailer.

Ingredients:

- 3 anchos
- 3 pasillas
- 3 *mulatos*
- 1 onion, finely chopped
- 3 garlic cloves, crushed
- 1 oz (30g) almonds, toasted
- 1 oz (30g) sesame seeds, toasted
- 1 tsp coriander seeds, ground
- 5–6 tomatoes, peeled

- 2 oz (60g) raisins
- 2 oz (60g) dark chocolate
- ½ cup (150ml) chicken stock
- 1 tsp cinnamon, ground
- sunflower oil
- 3–4 lb (1.5–2kg) chicken or turkey pieces
- black pepper to taste

Instructions:

Remove the stems and seeds from the chilies before heating in a dry frying pan for a few minutes. Keep them moving so that they don't burn, then rehydrate them in chicken stock for 10–15 minutes. Remove chilies from the stock, place in a blender with onion, garlic, sesame seeds, almonds, coriander seeds, cloves, cinnamon, and a little black pepper, and blend to a fine paste.

Slice peeled tomatoes in half, scoop out their seeds, and chop fine. Melt the chocolate in a double boiler. Heat some of the sunflower oil in a heavy pan and fry the raisins until they puff up. Remove from the pan when they start to brown, add a little more oil if necessary, and fry the paste you have made. Stir in the chicken stock you used to soak the chilies. Add the raisins and chopped tomatoes. Bring to a boil and gently simmer for 10–15 minutes. Add the melted chocolate, and your sauce is ready to add to the chicken or turkey.

In a frying pan, seal the chicken or turkey in a little oil. Place in an ovenproof dish, cover with the sauce, and bake at 356°F (180°C) for 30–40 minutes. Serve with plain boiled rice.

Tostadas

Most Mexican restaurants serve a version of *tostadas*, fried wheat tortillas with a layer of refried or kidney beans, chicken, lettuce, guacamole, sour cream, and grated cheese topped with pickled jalapeños.

Ingredients:

- 1 tortilla per person
- 1 can of refried or kidney beans, mashed
- lettuce cut into strips
- 1 chicken breast, cooked and flaked into pieces
- guacamole
- sour cream
- cheddar cheese, grated
- 2 jalapeños (pickled or fresh), chopped
- oil for frying

Instructions:

Fry the tortillas in hot oil, approximately 30–45 seconds per side. Flour tortillas will puff up when fried, but be careful not to let them brown or burn.

Place the fried tortilla on a plate and cover with a layer of beans (warmed if you like). Add the chicken, lettuce, and good dollops of guacamole and sour cream, and top with the grated cheese and chopped chilies.

Hot Juan's fajitas

Fajitas were traditionally made from cheap cuts of beef, cut across the grain into thin strips and marinated to tenderize them. Nowadays almost any meat can be used. The fast cooking seals in the moisture and keeps the meat very tender.

Ingredients:

- 2–3 chicken breasts, or ¾ lb (300g) beef
- 3–4 tsp Hot Juan's BBQ rub (see page 100)
- 1 red pepper, seeded and cut into strips
- 1 yellow pepper, seeded and cut into strips
- 1 large onion, finely sliced
- oil
- 10–12 wheat tortillas
- guacamole
- sour cream
- salsa

Instructions:

This recipe uses the dry spice marinade we created for barbecues. It is ideal for this type of fast, high-heat cooking, but it will not tenderize the meat. Cut the meat into strips, cutting across the grain of the meat. Place the meat in a bowl and sprinkle on some Hot Juan's BBQ rub, making sure you get an even coating.

Heat oil in a large frying pan and fry the meat over a high heat until it has browned. Set aside and fry the pepper and onion in the same pan. When they are almost done, return the meat to the pan and complete cooking. Doing this in two batches stops the pan from cooling down.

Spoon the meat in a warmed bowl and serve with warmed tortillas, guacamole, sour cream, and salsa.

Hot coconut plantains

In culinary terms, "plantain" refers to a green, unripe banana that is treated as and prepared like a vegetable. Sound strange? Try it—this recipe is superb.

Ingredients:

- 2 green plantains
- 3 ½ oz (90g) fresh coconut, grated
- 3 tbsp onions, finely sliced
- 1 or 2 green chilies, seeded and sliced
- 1 tbsp thick coconut cream
- salt
- dash of lime juice

Instructions:

Peel the plantains and boil them in lightly salted water until soft. Drain and mash, adding the coconut, onions, chilies, and coconut cream. Add salt to taste and a dash of lime juice. Serve with rice.

Curried water spinach

Water spinach should be thoroughly washed, as it grows in swampy areas. You can also try this recipe with ordinary spinach or cabbage.

Ingredients:

- 1 lb (500g) water spinach
- 2 tbsp oil
- sprig of fresh curry leaves
- 1 medium onion, finely chopped
- 2 tsp dry chili flakes
- 1 tsp salt

Instructions:

Wash water spinach, shake dry, and break into bite-size pieces, using only the leaves and tender tips of stems. Heat oil and fry curry leaves and onions until onions are soft and brown. Add dried chili, salt, and the water spinach. Heat for five minutes. Serve with rice.

Cincinnati fiveway chili

This is a real chili spice-fest, totally unlike the mincemeat-and-chili-powder version familiar to many of us.

Ingredients:

- 6–10 anchos
- 5–10 piquins
- 2 onions, finely chopped
- 5 garlic cloves
- 7 oz (200g) braising steak, cubed
- 5 oz (150g) black beans, soaked
- 1 small bunch cilantro (coriander) (root and stalks chopped and reserved; leaves finely chopped)
- 1 can tomatoes
- 2 tsp oregano
- 2 cinnamon sticks

- 2 or 3 bay leaves, fresh or dried
- 1 tbs molasses
- 1 tbs cider vinegar
- 2 cups (500ml) water

1 tsp each of the following:

- paprika
- cumin, ground
- coriander seeds, ground

½ tsp each of the following:

- allspice
- cayenne
- cloves

Instructions:

Soak the black beans overnight. Drain, place in a pan of water, and bring to a boil. Drain once again, cover with cold water, and bring back to a boil. Reduce to a simmer and cook until tender—the timing could vary from one to two hours, so check frequently.

While the beans simmer, remove the seeds from the anchos and soak them. Drain but reserve the liquid with its fine, rich flavor. Pulp the chilies in a blender until smooth.

Slowly cook the onions until golden brown, but don't allow them to burn. Add the garlic until soft, then the chopped cilantro (coriander) root. Turn the heat to medium and add the meat. When the meat has browned, add the remaining spices and stir to coat the meat thoroughly. Sauté gently for a few minutes, but keep stirring all the while to stop the spices from sticking and burning.

Add the chili purée and their soaking liquid, as well as the tomatoes. Drain the beans, rinse, and add, along with the water.

Place in an oven dish and bake in a medium-hot oven for about 2–3 hours. Check occasionally and add more water to prevent your dish from burning—it may develop quite a crust if you like it like that. The meat should be tender, almost dissolving, and the beans soft and velvety.

Add molasses or honey if you like it with that bitter sweetness—I add some cider vinegar for a sour dash. If you want to add even more heat, you can crumble the piquin chilies in at this stage, but beware! Serve with spaghetti, beans, chopped green (spring) onions, or cheese and crackers.

Sichuan fiery beef

For an authentic taste, try to find a good Chinese supermarket to supply some of the more unusual ingredients for this delicious recipe.

Ingredients:

- 2–3 celery sticks or green beans
- 3 green (spring) onions
- 1 lb (500g) lean steak
- 1 tbsp Shaoxing wine (or sherry)
- vegetable oil
- 1 tsp Sichuan pepper (there really is no substitute for this)

- 2 tbs chili bean paste
- 2 cups (500ml) stock
- 2 tsp dark soy sauce
- 3 tbs flour mixed with 3 tbs water
- a handful of dried chilies

Instructions:

Trim the fat off the beef and cut (against the grain) into thin strips. Marinate in the wine. Heat three tablespoons of oil in a wok until very hot.

Cut the chilies in half and fry in the wok along with the pepper. Sauté until fragrant and just beginning to brown (don't let them burn), then remove them but leave the oil in the wok. When the chilies are cool, chop very fine, almost to the consistency of paste, and keep for later. Reheat the oil.

Chop the celery, or green beans, as well as green (spring) onions into pieces a few inches long and add to hot oil. As soon as they begin to color, remove from the heat and reserve, keeping the cooking oil again.

Stir the flour mixture into the beef to make sure all the strips are well coated. Heat the wok once again, this time adding the chili bean paste. Cook for a minute or so until the oil is red and fragrant.

Then add the stock and bring to a boil. When it is boiling vigorously, add the beef and bring back to a boil. Add the Shaoxing wine and soy sauce to taste. Leave for a few minutes, stirring occasionally. Then transfer to a serving dish and add the vegetables to the mixture.

When you are ready to serve, spread the chopped chilies on top of the beef mixture. Clean and dry the wok and heat up a tablespoon or so of oil until smoking hot. Pour this over the top of the dish, which will sizzle and spit dramatically. If you're quick, you can bring it to the table while it is still sizzling.

Hot Juan's BBQ ribs

I have prepared racks of ribs more times than I care to remember. Each time I try something new, and, so far, this is my best and simplest method.

Ingredients:

- Hot Juan's BBQ rub (see page 100)
- 3–4 racks of pork ribs
- 4 ¼ cups (1l) apple juice or apple cider
- 5 tbsp cider vinegar
- juice of one lemon
- 1 bottle BBQ sauce

Instructions:

Remove the inside membrane from the rack of ribs before you marinate it. With the tip of a knife, locate the end of the membrane and lift a flap. Carefully gripping the flap with a dishcloth, pull the membrane away from the ribs.

Now place the ribs in a large baking dish and pour over the cider vinegar, lemon juice, and apple juice. Don't worry if it does not cover the ribs—we will be leaving them in the marinade for at least four hours in the fridge, and I recommend rotating them during this time.

After they have marinated, drain the ribs (retain the marinade for future use) and coat evenly with Hot Juan's BBQ rub. Massage in well.

Bake the ribs in a baking dish in an oven set to 249–300°F (120–150°C) for a few hours. Every so often you can spoon on a little of the reserved marinade.

When the ribs are ready, it is time to cover them with the BBQ sauce and return them to the oven for 10 minutes or until they get sticky. Best served with French fries and coleslaw.

Chili-brined pork chops

The aim of brining pork for six to 18 hours before cooking it is to make it much more succulent. With today's leaner pork cuts, we miss out on the fat basting the meat during cooking. Brining compensates for this loss in flavor.

Ingredients:

- ½ lb (240g) salt, or 2 oz (60g) per 4 ¼ cups (1l) of water
- 8 ½ cups (2l) water
- 8 ½ cups (2l) apple juice
- dried chilies
- 6–10 peppercorns
- 2 garlic cloves

Instructions:

Pour the water and apple juice into a large pot. Add the salt, chilies, garlic, and peppercorns. (Adding sugar or molasses to the brine mix will make it sweeter.) Bring to a boil and simmer for 10–15 minutes.

Cool, strain, and then chill before using the brine to marinate your pork. You can brine almost any cut of pork, but the thicker cuts need to be left in the brine for longer.

To marinate the pork, place chops in a large plastic container, cover with the brine, and place in the fridge for 4–6 hours. When you are ready to cook, rinse the meat in fresh water and discard the brine. Grill or barbecue as normal.

Hot Juan's patties

It may not be practical to make sausage at home, so prepare patties from this recipe instead. You could even shape the meat into a roll and coat with a little flour before cooking.

Ingredients:

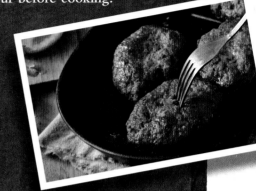

- 2–3kg lean pork
- 14–20 oz (400–600g) pork fat (ask your butcher for this)
- 2 oz (50g) Hot Juan's BBQ rub (see page 100)

Instructions:

Mince the meat and fat, place in a bowl, sprinkle on Hot Juan's BBQ rub to taste, and use your hands to mix until all ingredients are evenly distributed. It may be wise to wear household gloves, as the chilies could irritate your skin, especially if you have used a hot variety for your version of the rub.

Other ingredients, such as fresh or dried herbs, can be added to your mixture to enhance the flavor. If you don't like it too meaty, you can add bread crumbs or even boiled rice, but limit this to a maximum of 5–10 percent of the total weight of your meat mixture.

The flavor of the mixture will greatly improve if you are able to make it a few days before use, because the dry ingredients in the spice mix will have time to soak in.

Shape patties and roast on a barbecue over an open fire for the best results.

Chili mackerel

This simple dish makes for a quick and easy single-pan meal.
Serve it on a bed of rice or with fresh bread.

Ingredients:

- 4 mackerel fillets
- 4 fresh red chilies, seeded and chopped
- 1 oz (25g) blanched peanuts, unsalted
- 1 large red onion, chopped
- 2–3 garlic cloves, crushed
- 0.75" (1.5cm) square of ginger, finely chopped
- 1 tsp turmeric
- 1 tsp lemon juice
- 4 tbsp (50ml) olive oil
- 6 tbsp (75ml) rice wine vinegar, dry sherry, or chili sherry
- ¾ cup (175ml) water

Instructions:

Place all the ingredients—except the mackerel fillets and olive oil—in a food processor or blender and process until smooth. The mixture should not contain any large lumps, but it must not resemble a paste.

Add oil to a flat-bottomed frying pan, pour in the mixture from blender, and fry gently for a few minutes. Add the fish fillets and simmer on low heat for about six minutes, turning once.

Place fish onto plates and pour the sauce over it. You can serve this meal with French fries, rice, or fresh bread.

Spicy shrimp (prawns) with lime

Shrimp (prawns) are one of the most popular seafoods in the world. This recipe enhances their flavor and will delight your dinner guests.

Ingredients:

- 30 raw shrimp (prawns)
- 2 tsp fresh ginger, finely chopped
- 1 tbsp fish sauce
- 2 tsp brown sugar
- 4 green (spring) onions, sliced diagonally
- 4 red chilies, fresh

- 1 to 2 sticks fresh lemon grass
- 1 large onion
- 2 tsp galangal, finely chopped
- 1 tsp Thai pepper–cilantro (coriander) paste
- 2 tbsp peanut oil
- 3 tbsp coconut milk

- 1 tsp rice flour
- salt
- 2 lime leaves or lime rind
- red chilies, sliced for garnish

Instructions:

Shell the shrimp (prawns), but leave the tail intact. De-vein and use a sharp knife to slit each one lengthways from the top. Place in a bowl and mix in ginger, fish sauce, sugar, and green (spring) onions. Marinate for 10 minutes.

Remove the seeds from the chilies. Purée in a blender with galangal, lemon grass, onion, and Thai pepper–cilantro (coriander) paste.

Heat oil in a wok or frying pan. Add the paste mixture and stir-fry until fragrant. Add the shrimp (prawns) with marinade and simmer, turning constantly until they change color. Remove the pan from the heat.

Mix coconut milk with rice flour and heat in a saucepan, stirring until it boils and thickens. Add salt to taste, then pour into the center of a serving plate or bowl. Place shrimp (prawns) on sauce and sprinkle with thread-fine strips of lime leaves or rind and fresh chili.

Crab with chili

This is an excellent seafood dish prepared in true, exotic Singapore style to give your meal a very special touch.

Ingredients:

- 2 raw crabs
- ½ cup (125ml) peanut oil
- 2 tsp fresh ginger, finely grated
- 1 tsp garlic, finely chopped
- 3 red chilies, seeded and chopped
- 3 tbsp tomato sauce
- 3 tbsp hot chili sauce
- 1 tbsp sugar
- 1 tbsp light soy sauce
- 1 tsp salt

Instructions:

Clean the crabs. Remove hard top shell, stomach bag, and fibrous tissue. Chop the flesh in 2–4 pieces, depending on size.

Heat a pan and add oil. When hot, fry the crab pieces until they turn orange or red, turning to cook on all sides. When done, remove, turn heat low, and fry the ginger, garlic, and chilies, stirring constantly, until soft and fragrant. Do not let them brown.

Add the tomato sauce, chili sauce, sugar, soy sauce, and salt. When the mixture boils, return crabs to the pan and simmer for three minutes. If sauce reduces too much, add a little water. Serve with rice.

SNACKS AND SWEETS

Chili corn bread

This corn bread goes great with a barbecue and fresh salads. In winter it makes a perfect companion for rich tomato soup (any leftovers can be made into spicy croutons).

Ingredients:

- 5 oz (150g) finely ground polenta
- 5 oz (150g) self-rising (self-raising) flour
- 4 tsp baking powder
- ¼ tsp salt
- 2 oz (60g) superfine (caster) sugar
- 1–2 tsp paprika

- 2 chilies, finely chopped
- ¾ cup (200ml) milk
- 10 oz (300g) crème fraiche
- 2 medium eggs

Optional extras:

- 3 ½ oz (100g) strong cheddar cheese, grated
- 1 can sweet corn
- mixed herbs

Instructions:

Lightly grease a medium-sized, round cake pan (tin) and preheat the oven to 400°F (200°C).

Mix all the dry ingredients in a mixing bowl and add the chopped chilies. In a separate bowl, mix the milk, crème fraiche, and eggs, then add to the dry ingredients and blend using a whisk or mixer.

Pour the mixture into the cake pan (tin), place in the oven, and bake for approximately 30–45 minutes. When it is ready, the bread should be golden brown and firm to the touch.

For a different flavor, you can add either grated cheddar, sweet corn, or a pinch of mixed herbs.

Coconut flatbread

This exotic flatbread is made with freshly grated coconut, though desiccated coconut moistened with a few tablespoons of cold water can also be used.

Ingredients:

- 1 lb (500g) fine rice flour
- 1 tsp baking powder
- 3 oz (75g) coconut, freshly grated
- 2 tsp salt
- 2 tsp butter (use ghee if you can)
- 2 tbsp onions, very finely chopped
- 1 tbsp fresh chili, finely chopped
- 1 egg, beaten
- 2 cups (500ml) water
- ghee or oil for cooking

Instructions:

Mix the flour, baking powder, coconut, and salt in a bowl. Rub in the butter, stir the onions and chili through, and then add egg and water to make a dough. Leave to rest for half an hour.

Take egg-sized pieces of dough and pat between floured hands or roll lightly on a floured board to the size of a saucer. Cook on a hot stove in a preheated heavy frying pan lightly coated with oil.

Serve with curries or sambals.

Deviled omelet

If you are tired of the old mushroom-and-cheese, cheese-and-ham, ham-cheese-and-tomato variations, then try this spicy breakfast surprise.

Ingredients:

- 4 eggs
- 1 tbsp cold water
- salt and black pepper
- 1 tbsp butter or oil

- 3 tbsp chilies, sliced
- 3 tbsp onions, sliced
- 1 tsp dill, chopped

Instructions:

Beat the eggs and add cold water, salt, and pepper. Heat half the butter in a pan and fry the chilies and onions until soft. Cool the mixture, then stir it into the eggs together with the dill.

Reheat the pan, adding the remaining butter, and pour in the eggs. As the eggs set around the edge of the pan, draw the mixture to the center, tilting the pan so the raw egg runs to the edges. Fold and serve.

Empanadas

These small pastry turnovers can have a sweet or savory filling. We are going to cheat and use prepared shortcrust pastry, but if you wish to make your own pastry, then use chicken stock instead of water to mix your dough. You'll get a more authentic flavor that way.

Ingredients:

- 5 oz (150g) beef mincemeat
- 5 oz (150g) turkey or chicken mincemeat
- 1 large onion, chopped
- 1 red pepper, skinned, seeded, and chopped
- 1 garlic clove, puréed

- 2 chilies (fresh or rehydrated), finely chopped or puréed
- pinch of cloves, ground
- pinch of cumin, ground
- 1 tbsp tomato purée
- salt and pepper
- 2 lb (1kg) shortcrust pastry
- oil

Instructions:

Fry the onion and meat in a pan. Add the chilies and spices and fry for about five minutes. While the meat is simmering, roast the red pepper, remove its skin and seeds, and chop into small pieces. Add to the pan, together with the tomato purée. Simmer until enough liquid has evaporated so that the mixture will not run when put into the pastry parcels.

Roll out the pastry on a floured surface until it is an even thinness of about 0.1" (3mm). Cut out as many 3.5–4.2" (9–11cm) circles as you can (normally 15–20). Place enough of the filling on the circles so that you can still close the pastry by folding it in half. Dampen the edges of the pastry before sealing, and pinch the edges together using your fingers, a fork, or a special gadget.

In a deep fat fryer, large pan, or wok, heat 1–1.5" (3–4cm) of oil to 356°F (180°C). Remove finished pastries from the oil once they are golden brown, draining on a paper towel. Serve with salsa or hot chili sauce.

Gyoza dumplings

Provide chili sauce, soy sauce, and wasabi as dips.

Ingredients:

- ½ lb (250g) white fish, skinned and filleted
- juice of four limes
- 2 tbs rice wine vinegar
- a handful of chopped cilantro (coriander) leaves
- 1 chili, chopped
- ¼ white cabbage, chopped
- 1 small leek, chopped
- flour
- dumpling skins (Gyoza skins)

Instructions:

Place the fish, lime juice, rice wine vinegar, cilantro (coriander) leaves, and chopped chili in a bowl and marinate for two hours in the fridge.

Place the fish and marinade in a blender. Chop roughly and add the white cabbage and the leek. Blend to a chunky paste.

Flour a work surface or chopping board, place the dumpling skins on the surface, and put a teaspoon of the mixture in the middle.

Wet the edge of one half of the circle with your fingertips and then fold the dry side onto the wet side and squeeze the edges of the dumpling together. Pinch four points into the edge of the pastry and then, on the underside of each point, wet one half of the point only. Press the two sides together and you have a crease.

Drop the dumplings in boiling water in small batches. When they rise to the surface, fish them out with a slotted spoon and drain on a paper towel. Then heat some oil in a frying pan and fry them on one side until golden brown.

Serve with chili dipping sauce.

Flaming eggs in soy

This is one of the many varied ways of preparing eggs in Asia. Indulge yourself with this spicy meal that will make your mouth (and eyes) water.

Ingredients:

- 6 eggs
- 3 tbsp oil
- 1 medium onion, sliced thinly
- 2 chilies, sliced
- 2 tbsp brown sugar
- 3 tbsp water
- 2 tsp instant tamarind pulp
- 1 tbsp fish sauce
- cilantro (coriander) leaves

Instructions:

Boil the eggs until hard. Then remove from the heat and cool by running cold water into the pot. When cooled, remove the shells and dry. Pierce each egg with a toothpick and fry until golden and crisp. Drain on paper towels.

Pour off all but a tablespoon of the oil. Heat the pan again and stir-fry the onion and chilies until the onion is golden and slightly crisp. Then drain.

Mix the brown sugar, water, tamarind, and fish sauce. Stir the mixture over low heat until slightly thick. Pour the sauce over the eggs and sprinkle with the fried onion and chilies.

Garnish with cilantro (coriander) leaves and a chili flower. Serve with rice.

Hot Juan's potatoes

These make a great change from normal roasted potatoes, and if you cut them into thin slices instead of wedges, they are great with dips.

Ingredients:

- 3 tsp Hot Juan's BBQ rub (see page 100)
- ½ cup (150ml) olive oil
- 3–6 potatoes (medium size)

Instructions:

Mix the olive oil with Hot Juan's BBQ rub. Peel and slice the potatoes. Parboil and drain, then place in a mixing bowl and pour the oil mixture over, mixing until the potatoes are coated. Leave to marinate.

Pour a little olive oil in a roasting pan and preheat in oven set to 390–430°F (200–220°C). When hot enough, remove the pan from the oven, add the marinated potatoes, and return to the oven. Roast until golden and crispy, turning once or twice if you wish.

Pakora

This tasty, traditional Indian snack is probably the most commonly eaten treat, sold by street vendors and enjoyed all over India.

Ingredients:

- ½ lb (250g) chickpea flour
- 5 oz (125g) onions, chopped
- 1 cup (250ml) milk
- ½ cup (125ml) water
- ½ tsp sugar
- ½ tsp salt
- 2 chilies, finely chopped
- 2 tsp coriander seeds, ground
- 1 tsp cumin, ground
- 1 tsp turmeric, ground
- 2 cups (500ml) sunflower oil

Instructions:

Place all the ingredients—except the oil—into a bowl and mix well. Heat the oil and place teaspoon-sized balls of batter into the hot oil. Fry until browned and repeat until the batter is used up. Serve with curry and rice.

Stuffed anchos

This is another classic contribution from Derryck Strachan at the Ashburton Cookery School.

Ingredients:

- 4–6 anchos
- 3 or 4 tomatillos, chopped
- 1 small onion, chopped
- 2 tomatoes, chopped
- ½ cup (125ml) crème fraiche
- a handful of grated cheese (such as cheddar)
- all-purpose (plain) flour
- 2 eggs, separated
- oil for frying

Instructions:

Slit the anchos and remove the seeds, then toast them in a dry pan over medium heat for 30–90 seconds a side, before soaking in warm water for 10–15 minutes or until soft and pliable.

Meanwhile, heat some oil in a frying pan and fry the chopped tomatillos for around three minutes. Add the onion and cook for three minutes, then the tomatoes and cook for another three minutes. Stir in the crème fraiche and season. Cover and simmer until the mixture bubbles up, then remove from the heat. Beat the egg whites until they form stiff peaks, then stir the egg yolks in one at a time.

Heat enough oil in a frying pan to cover the chilies. Take the soaked chilies, carefully open the slit, and stuff with cheese. Turn them in the flour and then dip in the egg mixture to coat. Drop them straight into the hot oil without splashing. Fry one or two at a time, browning on each side. Drain on a paper towel.

Reheat the sauce and pour it over the chilies.

Chili chicken "popcorn"

This is my homemade, improved version of a commercially produced product. It is very quick and simple to make. The batter needs to be kept cool; it is best used chilled from the fridge.

Ingredients:

- 2–3 cooked chicken breasts
- 1 large egg
- ½ cup (100ml) water (cooled)
- ¼ cup (50ml) white wine vinegar

- 3 oz (80g) all-purpose (plain) white flour
- ½ tsp mixed herbs
- 1 clove garlic, crushed
- ½ tsp chili powder
- ¼ tsp black pepper, freshly ground
- oil for frying

Instructions:

Whisk the egg, water, and white wine vinegar together. Place flour, herbs, garlic, chili powder, and black pepper in a mixing bowl and gently stir with a whisk while adding the liquid. Mix well and store in the fridge ready for use.

Heat 1–1.5" (3–4cm) of oil to 356°F (180°C) in a deep fryer or large pan (wok). If you don't have a thermometer, the standard test is to drop a small cube of white bread into the oil and see how long it takes to brown (about 60 seconds is what we are looking for).

While the oil is heating, chop the chicken breasts into small cubes and mix them into the batter, making sure they are well covered. When the oil is hot, fry the chicken in small batches. Remove when golden brown, drain, and cool on a paper towel.

This chicken "popcorn" is great with dips.

Spicy cashews

These delicious nuts can be served as a savory snack with drinks. They are very tasty and bound to keep you coming back for more!

Ingredients:

- 1 lb (500g) raw cashew nuts
- oil for deep-frying
- 2 tsp chili powder
- 2 tsp salt

Instructions:

Heat oil in a pan and fry the cashews. Stir constantly with a slotted metal spoon. When pale golden, remove and drain on paper towels (the nuts will continue to cook in their own heat even after they have been removed from the oil). When all the nuts have been fried and drained, sprinkle with a mix of chili powder and salt. Toss well to distribute the flavors.

When cold, dust off excess salt and chili powder (shaking nuts in a colander is a good way to get rid of excess chili and salt) and serve. May be made a week or two before required and stored in an airtight container.

Hot cheese straws

Store-bought cheese straws are tasty but very expensive for such a simple product. Here is my version of this popular party food. The cheese straws are best when they are fresh, but don't worry—they won't have a chance to get very old.

Ingredients:

- ½ lb (250g) all-purpose (plain) flour
- ¼–½ tsp English mustard powder
- ½–1 tsp chili powder, finely ground (select your favorite variety)
- 5 oz (150g) butter
- 5 oz (150g) strong cheese, grated (cheddar is best)
- water
- salt and pepper

Instructions:

Preheat the oven to 400°F (200°C).

Sieve the flour, mustard, and chili powder with a little salt and pepper. Rub in the butter until the mixture resembles bread crumbs and then add most of the grated cheese. (Retain a little to sprinkle over the straws before baking.) Mix well, gradually adding enough water to make a firm dough.

Roll out the dough about 0.75" (4–6mm) thick on a floured surface. Sprinkle with the remaining cheese and cut into strips about 0.75" (2cm) wide. Place on baking parchment or a non-stick baking tray and bake for 10–15 minutes or until golden brown.

Cool on a wire rack and store in an airtight container.

Chili chocolate shots

From the beginning of history—well, at least since the Aztecs—chilies and chocolate have gone together. Today it would seem that sugar has replaced chilies, so how about a drink to revive the original pairing?

Ingredients:

- 3–4 pieces of chocolate per serving (at least 70 percent cocoa content)
- 1 good pinch of chili powder
- ½ cup (100ml) milk per serving

Instructions:

Melt the chocolate in a double boiler or in a bowl that has been placed in a larger bowl of hot water. Add a good pinch of chili powder and stir.

Warm the milk in a pan, add to the melted chocolate, and stir well. (You may need to return this to the pan if not all the chocolate has melted.) Serve in espresso cups.

An alternative method is to use a microwave oven to heat the chocolate and then the milk before combining them. Stir well before a final heating in the microwave. For an interesting variation, add a little espresso coffee to the mix, or even some brandy on a cold day.

INDEX

ABOUT THE AUTHOR

David Floyd's love for chilies stemmed from the many business trips he took to the United States, where his colleagues competed to see who could find the hottest dish for him to eat. He may have been defeated many times by the capsaicin, but his tolerance grew, as did his fascination for this most popular of spices. And so began his collection of chili recipes from around the world

David is an accomplished and adventurous cook, which has led him to create the Hot Juan range of snacks, along with an assortment of chili flavors that have been used to spice a host of different foods.

His products were sold through his business The Chile Foundry. He is a regular at the West Dean Chilli Fiesta, and chili aficionados make a beeline for his stand to discuss hot topics.

David has appeared on the BBC *Good Food Live* program, showing a number of chili varieties and inflicting some of his products on presenter Jeni Barnett.

The Chile Foundry converted to a blog and contained many thousands of articles about chilies. Unfortunately, the site has now closed, but David has continued to write chili chapters for books and specialist magazine articles.

Picture credits

Copyright rests with the following photographers and/or their agents.

All illustrations by Steven Felmore.

The following images are credited to Shutterstock.com and their respective creators: heat rating bars throughout: Yes - Royalty Free; front cover: lunamarina; back cover top: lunamarina; back cover bottom: StockImageFactory.com; 2: Irina Rostokina; 4–5: Krasula; 6: Jiri Hera; 17: MRAORAOR; 20: Marko Razpotnik Sest; 21: Anjo Kan; 24: Mikhail Martynov; 25: taboga; 26: Denphumi; 41 top: Anna Zakharchenko; 74: xpixel; 78: MagicBones; 86–87: Dream79; 88: showcake; 90: Swapan Photography; 91: grafvision; 92 top: Michelle Lee Photography; 92 bottom: Tanya Sid; 93: Fanfo; 95: Aleksandr Rybalko; 96 left: azure1; 96 right: Africa Studio; 97: StockImageFactory.com; 98–99: BriskAndBold; 99: rawf8; 100 left: PurMoon; 100 right: Dar1930; 101 top: baibaz; 101 middle: Tanya Sid; 101 bottom: grey_and; 102 top: Tim UR; 102 bottom: grafvision; 104: Larisa Blinova; 105: FPWing; 106: Larisa Blinova; 107 left: Africa Studio; 107 right: Aris Setya; 108: kannadhee; 109: nito; 110: jakkapan; 111: Fierman Much; 112–113: nafterphoto; 114: MaraZe; 115: Paulo Vilela; 116 top: AS Food studio; 116 bottom: azure1; 117: bonchan; 118 left: baibaz; 118 right: Hong Vo; 118 bottom: gowithstock; 120 top: Hong Vo; 120 bottom: Larisa Blinova; 121 top: Quang Ho; 121 bottom: Louno Morose; 123 top: etorres; 123 bottom: Enlightened Media; 124 top: robertsre; 124 bottom: paulista; 125 top: Swapan Photography; 125 bottom: muk woothimanop; 126 top: MaraZe; 126 bottom: Keith Mecklem; 127: AmyLv; 128: nickichen; 129: akepong srichaichana; 130 top: StudioPhotoDFlorez; 130 bottom: Africa Studio; 132: Sea Wave; 133: Pani_Elena; 134 top: Boonchuay1970; 134 bottom: Artit Wongpradu; 135: Foodio; 137 top: Aleksandr Rybalko; 137 bottom: Eric Isselee; 140 top: julie deshaies; 140 bottom: mahirart; 141 top: Iurii Kachkovskyi; 141 bottom: MariaKovaleva; 142: designs by Jack; 143 top: Rimma Bondarenko; 143 bottom: StockImageFactory.com; 145: StockImageFactory.com; 146: Justin Kaewnopparat; 147 top: Maks Narodenko; 147 bottom: Wolna; 148 top: Andrii Horulko; 148 bottom: Indian Food Images; 149: Olga Popova; 150: MaraZe; 151 top: Brian A Jackson; 151 bottom: Lotus Images; 152: Jiri Hera; 153: grafvision; 160: nattharit poungpath

Other image credits: 7: Photo Access; 8: David Floyd; 11: © Images of Africa/Dirk Pieters (www.imagesofafrica.co.za); 12: Digital Source; 14: Peter Bosman; 15: Gallo Images/Gina Martin; 16: Getty Images/Hulton Archive; 18: Gallo Images/Image Bank/Donata Pizzi; 22: © Images of Africa/Dirk Pieters (www.imagesofafrica.co.za); 23: Peter Bosman; 27: Photographers Direct/Nikhilesh Haval (nikreations@yahoo.com); 28: David Floyd; 30: © Images of Africa/Peter Blackwell; 33: Cephas/Stockfood; 63: © Images of Africa/Shaen Adey; 65: © Images of Africa/Roger Bell; 66: Photo Access; 69: © Images of Africa/Alain Proust; 71: David Floyd; 73: © Images of Africa/Dirk Pieters; 75: Cephas/Stockfood; 77: Cephas/Stockfood; 81: David Floyd; 83: © Images of Africa/Francois Hancke; 85: Digital Source; 89: Photo Access; 158: Cephas/Stockfood; 94, 103, 119, 122, 131, 136, 138–139, 144: iStock